How to cope with caring for my ill partner

Janet Haines
Mandy Matthewson

Acknowledgements:
Steven Haines
Robyn Cartledge
Coverart designed by Freepik
(www.freepik.com)

This workbook offers suggestions on how to cope when caring for an ill partner. We do not guarantee that these suggested strategies will resolve all psychological symptoms. You may wish to seek alternative assistance from a mental health professional.

How to cope with caring for my ill partner
Janet Haines & Mandy Matthewson
Copyright © 2025
ISBN: 978-1-923573-16-1

About the authors

Dr Janet Haines has a PhD in Clinical Psychology and has worked as an academic and researcher for 17 years, and in private practice for 30 years helping people facing life problems.

Dr Mandy Matthewson is a Clinical Psychologist, educator and researcher with more than two decades of experience supporting people through life's toughest challenges.

For AW and AP.
Your devotion is inspiring.

Table of contents

Table of contents 5
Introduction 7
Challenges being faced 8
    Increased workload 8
    Having to do things you have never done before 9
    You become the decision-maker 10
    Intrusions in your home 11
    Changes in your partner 11
    Grief 13
The obligations you feel 15
    Commitment to your partner 15
    Burden of responsibility 16
The problem of burnout 17
    What is carer burnout? 17
    Indicators of carer burnout 17
    Why does burnout happen? 19
    The impact of burnout 21
    What should you do? 22
What do I need to do to begin to cope? 25
    Recognise changes and losses and your reaction to them 25
    Change your attitude to taking control 25
    Take time out to consider your needs 26
    Introduce rewarding activities 26
    Do not react like every stressor is a crisis 27
    Build structure into your day 27
    Manage the effect of the pressures on you 27
    Use available resources 27
    Ask for and accept help 28
    The idea of respite 28
What should I do? 29
Develop a contingency plan for crisis situations 30
    A simple strategy to manage worry 33
Manage your anxiety 35

- Functioning of your nervous system 35
- Range of arousal 38
- Anxiety management strategies 39
- Quieting your mind 47
- Controlling your anger 52

Manage your disturbed sleep 53
- What can I do about my sleep problems? 55

Learn acceptance 57

Manage your emotional reactions 59
- Primary and secondary emotions 59
- Recognising and dealing with your emotions 61
- The link between your emotions and your behaviour 64

Find ways to cope 67
- Coping 67
- Problem-focused coping vs. emotion-focused coping 67
- Problem-approach vs. problem-avoidance copers 68
- Identifying your preferred coping style 71
- Building your coping repertoire 74

Manage your time 83
- Break down your high priority, important tasks 86
- Avoid distractions and deals 87
- How to make time when you seem to have none 87

Increase your life satisfaction 90
- Values clarification exercise for choosing preferred activities 90

Need for self-care 93

Additional reading 94

Introduction

The purpose of this workbook is to help you find ways to cope with the challenges you are facing caring for a partner whose health is deteriorating. This book should be useful for people who are feeling overwhelmed by the demands placed on them by their partner's health problems or for people who anticipate facing these problems in the future and are worried about how they will cope.

This workbook will focus on you and the challenges you face rather than your partner and the challenges related to the specific illness or health problems they are experiencing. This is because the illnesses partners could be experiencing are too many and varied to be covered in this workbook. Nevertheless, this workbook does look at general issues that come with an increasingly demanding role as a carer and support for your partner.

Challenges being faced

We shall begin by considering some of the challenges you are likely to be facing in caring for a partner with deteriorating health. We have considered these challenges in no particular order. Rather, we have tried to identify the types of day-to-day demands that can stretch your coping abilities.

Increased workload

Often, when your partner's health deteriorates, your day-to-day workload increases. There are two reasons why this occurs. Firstly, the demands on you increase because there is simply more to do. Focusing on health concerns, keeping track of medications, getting your partner to medical appointments, etc., all increase the number of things you have to do. These additional demands occur on top of the things you would normally undertake to run your household and your life.

The second reason your workload increases is because you often have to take on the tasks that previously would have been assigned to your partner. If they are no longer able to do as much or do things as well as they previously were able to do, or if they can no longer engage in any task that helps run your household, your workload is bound to increase. It is understandable that you would be the person to pick up these chores. So, instead of a shared workload, you become the primary or sole worker in your home.

Consider this example.

> *Jack's wife, Diana, developed cancer that had metastasised to her bones. Despite being in very poor health, Diana wanted to remain at home. She was in considerable pain, which was managed by strong medications. Jack was able to manage her medication with the assistance of a community nurse who visited briefly every day. Jack was employed and continued to work in his job although he had cut back his hours slightly. He was able to continue to work because he had good support from friends and family members who would sit with Diana while he was at work.*
>
> *Before Diana became too ill, Jack and Diana used to work as a team. He was the breadwinner in the household, took care of the garden and maintenance, and helped around the house when he was able. Diana was a good housekeeper. She liked to cook and keep the house organised. She also cared for her young grandchildren several days a week while their parents worked. After she got sick, Jack took on Diana's roles, including looking after the grandchildren when he was able. He wanted to do all these tasks to a standard that would please Diana. He would get up early in the morning after a night often disturbed because of Diana's pain. He would attend to Diana's needs and then pack himself a lunch for work. He wanted the house to be tidy before one of his supportive friends or family arrived to sit with Diana while he was at work.*

> *As soon as he returned from work, he would relieve the temporary carer and take over Diana's care. He would also do all the household tasks, such as laundry, cleaning and meal preparation. By the end of the evening, he would get Diana settled and then fall into bed exhausted, only to face a disturbed night, getting up to help Diana with her pain. Weekends were spent catching up on all the things he had not been able to do during his work week. Jack no longer played golf or caught up with his friends despite these being activities that he particularly enjoyed.*

Even if you are quite capable of doing each of these tasks, their sheer volume can leave you exhausted. Also, the extra duties cause an imbalance in your life that did not previously exist. That is, you may find that you no longer have any time to relax or engage in enjoyable activities that used to comprise your leisure time. This can be challenging as you do not get any 'downtime'. Instead, when one job is finished, another is usually waiting for you.

Having to do things you have never done before

Another challenge that comes from taking on tasks that your partner used to undertake is that you end up having to do things you have never done before or have not done for a long time. Often, in relationships, there are clearly defined roles. For example, one or the other of you may do the cooking, typically pay the bills, do the gardening, put out the garbage or change the lightbulbs. If your partner is no longer able to undertake their assigned roles, it typically will fall to you to do these things.

So, not only do you have to do more, but you also have to learn how to do things that you happily did not have on your list of things to do prior to your partner becoming ill. This can be stressful and, in some circumstances, can challenge your confidence in your capacity to cope. For example, to have to become the cook or the financial manager of your household, when you have not done these things before, can seem like an enormous challenge beyond merely the extra time it takes to regularly complete these tasks.

Consider this example.

> *Before he became ill with dementia, Phillip was the manager of his household. He managed the money and responsibly paid the bills. He knew when the car needed servicing and who to call if the electric pump on the water supply at their country home needed maintenance. He had been a very efficient and capable household manager. This had suited Elizabeth, his wife, very well. She was happy for him to handle these matters while she contributed in a multitude of other ways.*

> *As Phillip's health deteriorated, a problem developed. Increasingly, Phillip was unable to take care of these issues, and Elizabeth failed to learn how to do them. Although they had recognised that Elizabeth needed to learn how to do these things, they had tended to avoid the day when she would take over. Phillip had been reluctant to give up the role, and Elizabeth had never pushed the point regarding the need to learn these tasks. So, by the time Phillip was no longer able to do these things, Elizabeth was still not in a position to take over the roles. She did not know how to use online banking and, really, did not have much idea about how much money they had or how she could access it. She did not know when the bills became due or how to budget to pay for them. She dreaded the day something went wrong around the house because she had no idea who to contact. She was faced with having to learn to take over the management of the household without any training.*

You become the decision-maker

In addition to the demands of having to do more and having to learn to do things you have not done or had to do before, you may find yourself having to be the primary or sole decision-maker in your household. In many relationships, there is equity in decision-making. When decisions have to be made, you both contribute to that process. However, this can change as the health of your partner deteriorates.

> *After a heavy downpour, Caroline was informed that the guttering on the roof of their holiday home was leaking badly. She called in a repairman who gave her two options. She could either patch up the section of the guttering or she could replace the guttering entirely. He gave her the pros and cons for each decision. He gave her quotes for both options.*
>
> *When faced with such issues, Caroline would normally discuss the options with her husband, Andrew. They would discuss the matter and make a decision. This had always worked out well for them. However, Andrew was very unwell. Although there were times when he was more lucid and clear thinking, most of the time, the disease he had caused his thinking to become clouded. Caroline was no longer able to rely on Andrew's decision-making. Further, Caroline was reluctant to bother Andrew with something that would likely cause him to become upset as he could cope with very little these days.*
>
> *Caroline was paralysed by anxiety and indecision. She worried that she would make the wrong decision, even though she was capable of looking at the problem and resolving it. She just felt unable to do so without the support of her partner.*

To be put in charge of making the right decisions can be anxiety-provoking for some people. It may be easier to do this if you are making decisions that will affect only you.

However, it may evoke more anxiety when the decisions you have to make affect others, including your unwell partner.

Intrusions in your home

There may come a time, or that time has already come, when you need assistance in your home. This help might be from health professionals, such as community nurses, or from other support workers. Although this help is required, it can be an intrusion on your privacy. Having people coming and going can make your home feel like it is a more public place than you would prefer. This is the reason why some people reject the help they could have available to them even when they would benefit from that assistance.

Consider this example.

> *Julia's partner had significant mobility problems and some difficulties with communication due to his medical condition. Her partner, Paul, was a large man, tall and thickset. In contrast, Julia was petite. As a result, Julia struggled to assist Paul with his mobility problems, even using the aides with which they had been provided. Communication with Paul was time-consuming because of his symptoms, but Julia was patient, and they managed to cope. However, the time taken to communicate meant that Julia had less time available to do other chores.*
>
> *As a result of these problems, Julia and Paul had lots of support. A person would come once a week to do some cleaning. A support person would come to their home every morning to get Paul out of bed and showered. Another support person would come in the evening to settle Paul into bed. A community nurse would come every second day. An occupational therapist would visit every so often to assess Paul's needs and offer support when necessary. There was an arrangement for a physiotherapist to come and assist Paul about once a week. Friends and family dropped in to spend time with Paul and offer assistance to Julia.*
>
> *Julia longed for some peace and quiet.*

Changes in your partner

One of the greatest challenges you may face relates to changes in your partner's functioning or demeanour. This tends to have two sources. Firstly, the changes may be directly caused by the illness itself. These changes may occur in your partner's activity level, cognitive functioning, memory or in factors such as personality that can be affected by changes in the brain.

Consider this example.

> *Angela and Grant had a little dog they both adored. It was Angela's job to feed the dog. She enjoyed this role. After being diagnosed with a condition that was slowly destroying the connections in her brain, there were fewer and fewer things Angela could do, but she enjoyed still being able to take care of their dog.*
>
> *Grant reminded Angela to give the dog his breakfast. Angela went about this task. However, when Angela tried to process the task, she made a fundamental error. When she thought of breakfast, she thought of muesli. So, Angela set about preparing a bowl of muesli with milk and yoghurt for the dog. Grant walked into the room as their dog was finishing his surprise breakfast treat.*
>
> *Unfortunately, the muesli contained sultanas, which are very bad for dogs. A call to the vet was followed by expensive veterinary treatment and an upsetting time for everyone, including the dog. Grant knew that Angela would never have been irresponsible prior to her illness. He realised she had made a mistake but recognised that Angela could no longer be trusted to do basic jobs. After that, Grant always fed the dog or supervised Angela feeding the dog when she insisted on doing so.*

Secondly, the changes may relate to the way in which your partner is coping with their ill health. Such changes may be in mood, pessimism and negativity, and psychological dependence or the opposite, that is rejection and withdrawal.

Your partner's mood may be low, and they may seemingly experience little pleasure in activities or social interactions they used to find pleasurable. In turn, this can affect your mood, as can changes in your partner's level of negativity and pessimism about the future. It is difficult to remain cheerful and optimistic when there is an atmosphere of gloom in the home and when interactions with your partner are characterised by a general sense of negativity. Consider this example.

> *Robert had sympathy for his wife, Evelyn. He understood how difficult it had been for Evelyn to become ill. He knew she experienced pain that made it harder for her to cope with what she was facing. However, his understanding of what she was going through did not make it easier for him to cope with her changed behaviour.*
>
> *Before her illness, Evelyn had been an easy-going person who was kind and thoughtful of others' needs. Since her illness had progressed, Evelyn had become increasingly severely critical of others, including Robert. She was dissatisfied with what others tried to do for her and could be brutal in the verbal attacks she would direct at people who annoyed her. She disregarded the needs of others and would become furious if her behaviour change was raised with her. Day in and day out, Evelyn ranted about her situation. She refused to seek help with her mood, blaming others for their failure to understand and care for her properly. Robert tried hard but found it very difficult to cope with the changes in his wife.*

Also, the way in which your partner responds to you may change. They can develop a strong sense of dependence on you. This is not only in relation to their need for you to do things for them. It may also relate to their need to have you around them all the time, being more demanding on your time than they may have been in the past. They may question you about what you are doing, where you are going and when you will be back. This can feel overwhelming at times.

Consider this example.

> *Jillian's mother used to say that her children 'drove her to distraction' being 'under her feet' all the time. Jillian now knows what she meant. Her previously self-sufficient and independent husband, Dean, had changed since he became ill. Jillian can barely leave his presence for any time at all before Dean calls her back. He wants to know what she is doing all the time and becomes anxious and unhappy if she has things to do that take her away from him. There are some things that Jillian can't avoid doing that take her away from the home. However, she faces a dilemma. Dean does not accept anyone else coming to stay with him when Jillian has to go out, even family and friends. He only wants Jillian. On Jillian's part, she tries to be sympathetic and understands that Dean is anxious. However, she is desperate for a minute to herself.*

In contrast, a partner with whom you used to have a close relationship can become withdrawn and reject you. They no longer share their thoughts and are less likely to want to engage in conversation with you and in shared activities. This can make you feel isolated and lonely.

Grief

The deteriorating health of a partner can cause you to feel a sense of grief in three ways. Firstly, you can grieve the loss of the things that you used to have but no longer have because of your partner's ill health. Secondly, you can experience a sense of grief in relation to the things you expected to have in the future that you now know are no longer available to you. This might be related to expectations you had or plans you made for the things you were going to do. Finally, you can experience what is known as anticipatory grief. If your partner's illness is likely to shorten their life, you can anticipate their death and grieve in advance for the loss of your partner.

Consider this example.

> *Thomas met, fell in love with, and married Georgia. She was an outgoing and vivacious woman who loved to laugh out loud at the absurdities of life. She was kind and generous, and Thomas adored her.*
>
> *When she was 39 years of age, Georgia had a stroke. She survived but was changed by the injury to her brain caused by the stroke. Georgia is now morose and disinterested in life. She is often critical of others and never sees the humorous side of life. Thomas has been told by Georgia's doctors that this will not change. Thomas' commitment to the woman he fell in love with and married motivates him to persevere despite Georgia's ambivalence about him and his presence. Thomas mourns the loss of the woman he loved.*

All of these challenges have the capacity to make you feel overwhelmed. Each one represents a demand on you to rise to the demands of the situation and cope with your reaction to them. However, the way you deal with these challenges can be influenced by another factor, that is, the obligations you might feel.

The obligations you feel

In addition to the aforementioned challenges you can face in dealing with the deteriorating health of your partner, there are certain obligations you may feel that can complicate how you cope with the changes in your life situation.

Commitment to your partner

Your commitment to your partner can cause you to choose to do things that are not necessarily in your own best interests. For example, it may cause you to persevere in an intolerable situation to ensure that you give your partner what you have undertaken to do. Consider this example.

> *When Jim was diagnosed with Alzheimer's, he discussed with his wife what he wanted for the future. He told Suzanne that he did not want to go into a nursing home. He told her he wanted to die at home. At the start of their journey with dementia, Suzanne agreed and promised her husband she would care for him at home.*
>
> *However, the reality of Jim's deteriorating health was more difficult than they could have imagined. Jim's illness had progressed to the point where the challenge of caring for him was exceeding Suzanne's capacity to cope. He was often confused. He would let himself out of the house when Suzanne's back was turned, and a number of times, he had gone missing. Suzanne had been forced to obtain help from the police. He had flooded the bathroom when he decided to fill the bath, but then, forgetting what he was doing, he wandered off. He was sometimes violent when he was confused and distressed, and he had hit Suzanne when he lashed out. His sleep was disturbed, and Suzanne rarely got an adequate amount of sleep. The number of problem situations just kept increasing.*
>
> *Despite already being stretched to her limit, Suzanne knew that things were going to get worse. She knew Jim's health would deteriorate further, and she would have to care for all of Jim's physical needs, and he would become bedridden. She dreaded things becoming more demanding than they already had become.*
>
> *At a time in her life when she should be slowing down and doing more of what she enjoys, Suzanna was overwhelmed by the demands on her. Jim's doctors, their family and friends have all told Suzanne that Jim needs 24-hour a day care that she cannot provide. They have all encouraged her to have Jim cared for in a well-equipped facility where his needs can be met. However, Suzanne had promised Jim that would never happen. Despite her despair, Suzanne felt she could not go against Jim's wishes and place him in care.*

Burden of responsibility

This felt obligation can create an excessive burden of responsibility for you. For example, you may feel responsible for the outcome of events over which you have little or no control, or you may take on more than you can manage. Consider the following example.

> *David took his commitment to his partner seriously. When he married Marian he promised to care for her 'in sickness and in health'. When Marian became ill, he reminded himself of that commitment and adopted his new role as her carer in a way that few could criticise. He was always there for her, and he tried to meet her every need.*
>
> *David's family and friends could see that he was struggling to cope. They encouraged him to accept some help in looking after Marian. David rejected their offers of help and their advice about taking advantage of outside services. His family and friends worried about what was going to happen to David as the demands on him further increased, as they were bound to do. But David was insistent that he would do this on his own because that is what he undertook to do when he married Marian.*

With the challenges you face that are compounded by your sense of obligation and burden of responsibility, you are likely to be in need of finding ways of coping with these demands.

The problem of burnout

Before considering ways to help you cope with the effects on you of dealing with your partner's deteriorating health, it is worthwhile considering the nature of carer burnout, its impact on you and ways you can help manage its effects. When we use the term carer, we are referring to anyone who adopts a caring role for a loved one, even if they are not formally identified as a carer.

What is carer burnout?

Carer burnout refers to the experience of the physical and psychological exhaustion that develops when you are overburdened and overwhelmed by the caring demands being placed on you, even if you take on these challenges willingly and with love. These caring demands exceed the resources you have to cope, including your personal resources such as optimism and stamina. As a result, your wellbeing is affected, as is your capacity to act in a caring role.

Indicators of carer burnout

There are a range of indicators of burnout that you should be aware of so you can recognise what is happening to you. Being able to identify the indications that burnout is developing will increase the chances you will act early to protect yourself when these indicators first appear.

Physical indicators of carer burnout

A number of physical problems can develop as a consequence of burnout. All of these are indicators of excessive stress levels and are related to changes in your emotional state. Fatigue is a common indicator of burnout. As you reach a point of burnout, you can feel increasingly exhausted and lacking in energy. The fatigue you feel can make it difficult to undertake even ordinary daily activities.

The sleep disturbance you can experience as a function of burnout, in part but not entirely, can account for the fatigue you feel. Excessive stress creating high nervous system arousal levels and stressful thoughts can keep you awake at night or interrupt the pattern of your sleep. Coping with the demands during the day is made more difficult by having a sleep disturbed night.

Excessive muscle tension that comes with being too stressed can start to cause muscle pain and tension headaches. These can be debilitating and make it more difficult for you to undertake your day-to-day activities.

You may experience gastrointestinal disturbances that are caused by changes in your nervous system arousal. Not only can these problems cause unpleasant symptoms, they can also affect your appetite and your weight.

Importantly, the enduring stress caused by burnout can make you vulnerable to developing frequent illnesses. This is because ongoing, heightened stress can affect how well your immune system functions. With a poorly functioning immune system, you are more prone to catching bugs and viruses to which you are exposed.

Emotional indicators of carer burnout

The experience of burnout is associated with a range of heightened emotions. These can be a confusing array of emotional states that can change depending on the situation you are in or the thoughts you are having at the time.

These emotional states include intense anxiety. There can be an underlying anxiousness present that can exacerbate in intensity from time to time. You can experience anxiety in relation to specific aspects of your situation or the anxiety can be more generalised and seem to be unrelated to any specific event.

You may experience mood swings, from periods of low mood to a heightened agitated state, characterised by increased irritability. The swings in your mood can make it difficult to be certain how you are going to feel on any day.

You may also experience feelings of frustration about specific challenges you face and resentment about your situation. These feelings may manifest as anger that is either directed at yourself or others, including your partner.

Psychological indicators of carer burnout

There are a range of other indicators of the presence of burnout. For example, you may socially withdraw and become isolated. The challenges of dealing with the normal demands of social engagement can seem to be too much to manage so you avoid them when you can.

Burnout can be associated with problems with your attention and concentration. This is because of your heightened nervous system arousal that occurs with prolonged stress.

There are a number of reasons for these problems with attention and concentration. The first relates to cognitive load. This means that you have too many things to think about at once when you are faced with the challenges of caring for the needs of your partner and when you are trying to perform the tasks that caring involves. Your brain tries to give them all some attention. This reduces how much attention can be directed at any one thing. Even when you try to concentrate on one thing, your brain still recognises you have other things on your mind that demand your attention.

Attention and concentration problems also can develop because this cognitive load causes you to experience intrusive thoughts about things that are not currently of central concern to you, such as performing a particular task. With your brain trying to keep track of everything that is going on, you will be distracted by 'reminder' thoughts that are a reflection of the fact that you have so many things you need to keep in your mind.

Another reason you experience attention and concentration problems when you are stressed is that your brain has what is known as attentional bias. That is, it pays attention to the things that are most important to your survival. Your brain pays attention to the fact that you are experiencing heightened levels of stress and reacts as if this stress is an indicator of imminent harm to you. With a survival bias, your brain may draw your attention to things that seem particularly stressful or cause you to focus on how you are feeling rather than on what you need to be doing.

Finally, attention and concentration problems are caused by the impact of prolonged stress on your executive functioning. The processes that take place in your brain that help you plan, organise and set goals and work towards them are known as your executive functioning. Prolonged stress reduces what is known as attentional control making it harder to filter out things that can distract you, such as all the other things you need to do or your worry about your partner's health. This causes you to have trouble concentrating and it causes you to overestimate threat. In this way, you perceive things are more immediately threatening than they actually are when you are just going about your daily routine and trying to get tasks done.

Problems with executive functioning caused by prolonged stress also interfere with your ability to engage in goal-oriented behaviour. You find it harder to set goals and pursue then in an effective manner. Prolonged stress also affects your decision-making abilities, and it becomes harder to know what to do when faced with choices. You can also experience problems with self-regulation, making it harder to keep good control of your emotional state, your thoughts and your actions.

Why does burnout happen?

There are certain things that will increase the risk of developing burnout. It is not only that these factors exist. It is also that they endure over time. It is the unrelenting nature of the demands on you that contribute to the burnout occurring.

Too many demands

The sheer volume of things you have to do can cause you to burn out. You can be overwhelmed by the fact that every day there are a multitude of urgent and time-consuming demands on you. The demands on you can also be excessive because of the challenges complex physical illnesses can create. So, the combination of too many things to do, long hours when you attend to these tasks, and the fact that the tasks relate to complex care needs can exceed your capacity to cope and burnout may occur.

Too few resources

A contributor to the development of burnout is the inadequacy of the supports you have available to look after your partner's needs. If you have too little help, you are likely to find it difficult to take time for yourself and to take time to rest.

Having too few resources might also relate to being stretched financially. This can place an added burden to you, especially if you have to make choices about how you spend limited funds. It is likely you would attend to your partner's needs before your own so that you are the one is impacted.

A consequence of having too little support is that you are then unlikely to be able to take adequate breaks to recuperate from the effects of the demands being placed on you. It may be that you do not have someone who can give you a chance to take time away from your caring duties, including longer terms breaks. Without respite, you are likely to leave yourself vulnerable to the development of burnout.

The nature of your partner's condition

Your partner's condition may present you with particular challenges that can seem overwhelming. These challenges might relate to the nature of the condition and the caregiving demands the condition presents. For example, caring for a partner whose condition means they cannot be left alone can place additional demands on you.

The deteriorating nature of a condition can be overwhelming, both in terms of physical demands and psychological impact. Knowing that things are not going to get any better can leave you vulnerable to the development of burnout.

Further, conditions that cause fundamental changes in your partner or cause significant impacts on your relationship can result in you experiencing additional stress. For example, some conditions can change a person's personality or alter the way they interact with others. These changes in people suffering from the condition can be difficult for the people who love them.

Expecting too much of yourself

If you approach the care of your partner with the expectation that you will be and should be the person who attends to all their needs, you will leave yourself vulnerable to burnout. In all likelihood, if you try to do everything, you will fail or be overwhelmed by the enormity of the demands on you. This can affect the way you view yourself. Feelings of inadequacy and unworthiness can develop.

Social isolation

When all of your time is devoted to the care of another, there is little time for activities that would be of lower priority than caregiving demands. For example, social activities, spending time with friends, and engaging in leisure activities are likely to be abandoned because they seem unimportant in comparison with care tasks. With increasing social isolation, your vulnerability to the development of burnout can increase.

The impact of burnout

You need to consider the importance of avoiding burnout or managing it if it occurs. You can understand this importance by examining the impacts of burnout if it develops.

Physical and mental health

Burnout can make you unwell, both physically and mentally. For example, the chronic stress that underlies burnout can have a detrimental effect on heart health. It affects your immune system functioning which can leave you vulnerable to the experience of a range of illnesses.

Burnout can significantly impact on your mental health. It has been associated with depression and anxiety. These symptoms make it more difficult for you to cope with the demands of caring for an ill partner.

Quality of caregiving

It is important to protect yourself from burnout or manage it if it occurs because it can have a detrimental effect on your care giving. When you consider the indicators of burnout, for example, the exhaustion, anxiety and anger, it is not surprising that the experience of burnout would affect your ability to care for your ill partner. In this way, burnout can reduce the quality of the care you provide.

Even more concerning is the impact burnout has on your capacity to meet the demands of the situations you face. You may find yourself neglecting the needs of your ill partner because your capacity to function well has been affected.

Relationship stress

It is acknowledged that dealing with the consequences of the condition your partner is facing can impact your relationship. There are the effects of changing roles and the challenges of the illness itself that can impact how your relationship functions. However, on top of that, burnout itself can place an additional strain on even the closest of relationships.

The effects of burnout can change your tolerance of irritations and can cause you to want to withdraw to protect yourself from further stress.

In addition, burnout can affect your relationships with family and friends. When the pressure on you exceeds your capacity to cope, you are likely to have little energy left over for the demands of social engagement. When people are faced with those sorts of pressures, they tend to withdraw because any social interaction uses more energy than they have available to them. It is hard to be engaging and friendly when your mind is focused on the stress you are experiencing.

What should you do?

There are ways you can both protect yourself from the development of burnout and manage it if it occurs. As you work your way through the rest of the workbook, you will find strategies you can learn to directly address the particular things you need to do to either prevent the development of burnout or manage it if you are experiencing it.

Self-care

The importance of self-care cannot be underestimated. You cannot care for your ill partner if you find yourself unable to cope. It is easy to prioritise your partner's needs over your own. Their needs seem immediate and yours seem like they can wait until you have a moment to attend to them. However, by always placing your needs down the list of important things to consider, you run the risk of never attending to them.

It is interesting that advice to caregivers always emphasises self-care but it is the advice most likely to be ignored. This is not necessarily because you do not think self-care is important. It is more likely that you rate other concerns more highly than your own well-being. However, by ignoring your needs, you are increasing the chance that you will experience burnout and be less able to care for the person whose needs you have prioritised.

Seek support

It is important to build a good support network for yourself to avoid developing burnout or managing it if it occurs. A support network can be comprised of people you can turn to for emotional support. These people might be family and friends but may also include professionals who have the skill to provide you with the support you need. However, it also should include people who can ease your burden and people you trust to whom you can hand over responsibility for looking after your partner when you need to step back and attend to your own needs.

Take breaks

You cannot function in top gear and expect to be able to sustain that level of energy and attention over an extended period of time. No one can. You need to have periods when you can relax and reduce your elevated nervous system arousal level. Otherwise, you continually function at the upper level of your tolerance for stress. If any additional challenge occurs, as often is the case when you are dealing with an illness, you have no flexibility to respond to the demands of the new situation because you are already at the extreme upper limit of your ability to cope.

To manage the development of burnout, you need to build regular breaks into your routine, as a matter of priority. You cannot be there for your partner if your own physical and mental health is compromised. Without periods of recovery for you, you will not be able to sustain your care over time.

Adopt reasonable expectations

You are not a superhero. You are not a machine. You cannot do what is beyond human capacity to do. To protect yourself from burnout or manage it if it develops, you need to be realistic about what you are able to achieve.

By setting unrealistic expectations, you are setting yourself up to fail. By setting moderate expectations, you are making it possible to manage the challenges you face. Moderate expectations allow you to care for your partner and look after yourself. By looking after yourself you are also benefiting your partner because you are increasing the chances that you can more comfortably deal with the challenges of the situation you are facing and to sustain that effort over time.

Stress management

Dealing with the issues that arise from caring for an ill partner is stressful. If you are feeling stressed, do not ignore that feeling. Ignoring it will not make it go away. As your stress level elevates, it increases the effect on your functioning and reduces your capacity to fulfil the roles you have taken on.

It is a good idea to build into your routine easy stress management techniques. If you adopt stress management as an essential component of your day, you can create a means of managing the impact of the pressure you are facing.

Seek assistance

If it becomes apparent that you have developed the symptoms of burnout, treat it like a health crisis. Focus on the strategies you can learn to manage those symptoms. If those strategies are insufficient to reduce the severity of your burnout symptoms, seek professional help. There are people available to help you. Do not assume that the symptoms will just go away if you keep pushing forward.

What do I need to do to begin to cope?

To meet the demands that occur when caring for your partner whose health is deteriorating, you need to consider what you need to do to cope with these demands. Most often, people just continue to do what they are doing and hope for the best. Alternatively, they can put their head down and just try harder. Neither of these options works very well in the long run.

It is important to recognise that there is a point that can be reached that would exceed everyone's coping capacity. At these times, it is necessary to develop new skills or enhance existing skills so that you can cope in a way that protects you without having a negative impact on your partner.

We will be considering ways to manage the challenges you are facing or will face in the future. In the meantime, there are some things you need to do.

Recognise changes and losses and your reaction to them

When the health of your partner is deteriorating over time, nothing stays stable. Your partner's situation and your own tend not to get better or, at least, stay better for long periods. As a result, your life feels like it is in a constant state of change.

This can occur in two ways. There can be an insidious decline in your partner's health. It is only when you compare your current situation to how things were, even a few months prior, that you fully appreciate how the situation is changing. The pressures on you continue to increase, but you are less aware of their immediate impact.

Alternatively, the pattern of deterioration can take the form of a serious and significant change followed by a plateau and then another significant change. This tends to make you feel like you are moving from one crisis to the next and the next without substantial adjustments being able to be made along the way. Pressures continue to be increasingly experienced as you deal with the changes.

When your partner's health deteriorates, you experience additional challenges that need to be addressed. You need to make adjustments to cope with these additional demands. These demands are not only the physical demands of caring for an ill partner. It is important for you to identify your emotional reactions to these changes and to find ways to deal with these reactions. We will discuss coping strategies later in this workbook.

Change your attitude to taking control

It is fair to say that most of us like to feel in control of the things that are happening to us. Unfortunately, when things are constantly changing, it is hard to feel the degree of control that you would prefer.

It can be the case that, in an effort to control things more, the focus is placed on the wrong things. You can end up expending a lot of effort and energy trying to control things that simply cannot be controlled or to change things that cannot be changed.

Your focus needs to be on controlling things you can control rather than the things you cannot. Your focus also needs to be on controlling things as they occur rather than trying to control the 'big picture' or controlling things that have not yet occurred. You can learn to set reasonable expectations for control. We will teach you some skills in this regard later in this workbook.

Take time out to consider your needs

It is easy for your own needs to move down your priority list when you are caring for your partner who is experiencing declining health. When there are other important things that make demands on your energy and time, it is simpler to give up the things that only affect you. However, your partner's well-being cannot be the only thing you are focusing on. You cannot only focus on their ill health and all the other demands on your time that flow on from their poor health. It is too emotionally and physically draining to have these things as your only or primary focus. You need to take time out in a way that will allow you to give some consideration to your own needs and your own well-being. We will be discussing this later in this workbook.

Introduce rewarding activities

As stated, there is a need for you to take time out to allow for things in your life that do not relate to your obligations towards others. Given that your available time is limited, it is very important that you do things you value rather than just fill in your free time, if any exists.

It is so easy to fill in any time you make by catching up on jobs you have not had time to do. This offers you little other than relief that the jobs are finally done. It certainly does not make you less exhausted or give you moments of peace. You should aim for a balance between the demands on your time and the things you would like to do to increase the quality of your life.

We do understand that it can seem impossible to even consider finding time to do things for yourself, especially when every moment of your day is filled with demands. Later in this workbook, we will focus on managing your time to allow you to take some time for yourself. We will also focus on identifying the things you could do that would most positively affect your quality of life.

Do not react like every stressor is a crisis

It is an easy trap to fall into to be so on edge that you react to every difficult situation like it is a crisis. It puts you in a permanent state of 'red alert' that is uncomfortable and unhealthy. You end up spending your days waiting for the next crisis to occur.

Rather than allow this to happen, you should consider, in a general sense, what is likely to happen and then develop a contingency plan. Such a plan would have a general outline of what to do if any one of a number of events happens. Then, rather than worrying about the next crisis, you can be assured that your plan is in place for what you have to do if such a particular thing occurs.

Even if you have to make minor adjustments to what you actually do at the time, you still have a general idea of what to do and how to do it already in place. We know that you cannot predict the future, so do not try. Just think in general terms about what you would need to be doing in certain circumstances. We will tell you how to develop a contingency plan later in this workbook.

Build structure into your day

Most people cannot function well in the midst of chaos. You might be able to manage it for a while, but it is difficult to cope with if chaos is your permanent state. With lots of demands on your time and appointments to attend, some people do better if there is structure in their day or week.

By building structure into your days and weeks, you can better assure that there are busy times and times to rest and relax. There are ways this can be achieved. We will be discussing this later in the workbook when we explore time management techniques.

Manage the effect of the pressures on you

You need to learn to manage your stress. The constant pressures on you cause a change in your nervous system arousal. This can make you feel quite uncomfortable and cause you to feel like you can no longer cope.

These constant pressures push your nervous system arousal outside of a comfortable range where you function the best. We will be educating you about your nervous system and its link to feelings of anxiety and stress. We will teach you ways to reduce your arousal to a more manageable level, including strategies that you can use if your sleep is disturbed.

Use available resources

You should use all the resources you have available to you to cope with the challenges of caring for a partner with deteriorating health. Understanding your preferred style of coping and building on the strategies you use to cope with problems and demands will assist you in coping with the additional challenges you face. We will cover coping and coping styles later in this workbook.

Ask for and accept help

You should realise that it is all right to ask for and accept assistance. You have the same right to that help as anyone else. Despite this, many people do not think they have a right to access help, that they would rather be independent despite being overwhelmed, and think they should be able to manage without assistance. With services available that would make your ability to cope easier, it seems appropriate to ask for and accept help.

The idea of respite

Sometimes, it is necessary to take a break of more than a couple of hours. This raises the issue of respite. We are referring here to having someone come into your home so that you can have some time away or placing your partner in care so that you can have a rest. Many people reject the idea of respite. We accept that this may not be what you want or your partner wants. However, it is worth bearing in mind that respite may become necessary if your well-being is to be maintained.

These factors are ones that you need to consider to begin to move towards coping with your situation. We now need to focus on the specific ways you can deal with these challenges.

What should I do?

So, what can you do to cope better with the challenges that come with your partner's deteriorating health? It is our intention here to teach you some skills that should help you cope and make your life easier.

In the upcoming sections, we will teach you to understand your nervous system and help you find ways to manage your stress. We will consider the need to develop a contingency plan for crisis situations so that you do not have to worry about things that may happen in the future. We will help you gain acceptance of the changes in your life as well as managing your emotional reactions to these changes.

Further, we will help you investigate your preferred style of coping and teach you ways to build up your coping skills. Given the demands on you, we will teach you ways to manage your time. This should help you find a way to put more valued activities into your life and improve your life satisfaction and quality.

Develop a contingency plan for crisis situations

It is easy to find yourself constantly worrying about things that might happen in the future. You can torment yourself about whether or not you will know what to do when these things happen. This worry causes you to anticipate everything as if it is going to be a crisis that will overwhelm you.

To understand how worry works, let's consider this simplified version of a worry model in the diagram below. You experience intrusive worry thoughts. These relate to possible future threats to yourself or others you care about. Then, a cycle of worry develops where you keep re-evaluating the threat, reaching the same conclusion that the threat is real or possibly real. No matter how many times you go over it, the threat continues to play on your mind. Of course, this causes you to feel anxious.

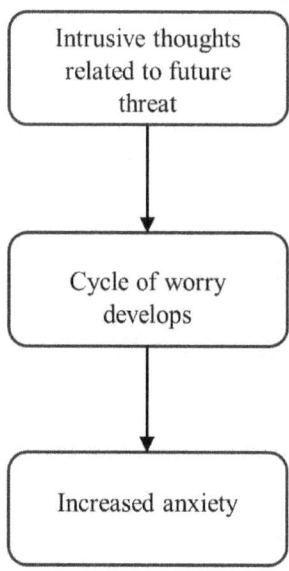

Figure 1: The relationship between thoughts, the cycle of worry and anxiety.

Looking more closely at this cycle of worry, what you do when you are worrying is outlined in the diagram below. When you have intrusive thoughts about a potential problem situation, you make some attempts to control that worry. Of course, if you could control your worry, you would simply do that. As a result of the worry being unpleasant, you search for some relief. But all your efforts to stop this process fail and your worry remains. You then start to worry that you are worrying. You then go back to trying to control your worry… and so on.

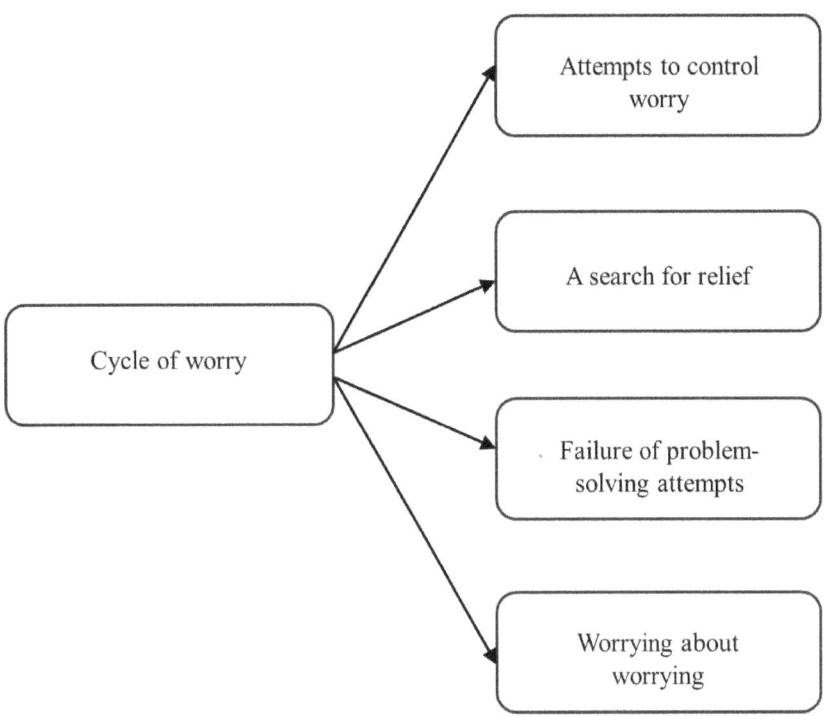

Figure 2: The components of the cycle of worry.

One way to stop this process is to develop a contingency plan of what you would do in certain circumstances. This contingency plan relieves you of the need to endlessly worry about things that might happen as you already have a plan in place for what you would do if the problem arises. When you start to worry, you can remind yourself of your contingency plan and, hopefully, let the worrying thoughts go.

This contingency plan can be expanded to contain information about what to do, who to contact, and lists of information that might be needed if someone had to take over from you, for example, if you became unwell.

Below is an example of what could be contained in a contingency plan.

Table 1: An example of a contingency plan for problem situations.

Example of contingency plan

Contact numbers:
    Doctors
        Dr Warman Caring, GP [enter phone number]
        Dr Nos A lot, Specialist [enter phone number]
    Neighbour
        Bob and June [enter phone number]
    Family members
        Daughter [enter phone number]
        Son [enter phone number]
        Sister [enter phone number]
List of medication and dosages
    Name of medication
        Dosage
        How often
List of other contact people and addresses
    Support person [enter phone number]
    Private ambulance service [enter phone number]
    Physiotherapist [enter phone number]
    Chemist [enter phone number]
    Electrician [enter phone number]
    Plumber [enter phone number]
    Handyman [enter phone number]
    Gardener [enter phone number]
    Mechanic [enter phone number]

> What to do if…
>
> > What to do if a medical emergency happens. *I will definitely call an ambulance. I am not in a position to know what to do, and that is the quickest way for us to get the medical assistance we need.*
>
> > What to do if I become concerned about my partner's health but it is not an emergency. *I will immediately call the GP practice and arrange for an appointment.*
>
> > What to do if I get sick. *I will contact [name] to organise some help. I will get out the list of my partner's medications and the other lists I have prepared of the things that have to happen to make sure my partner is cared for.*
>
> What to do if I need immediate assistance. *I will call Bob and June from next door who have offered to help me.*

Remember that not everything you worry about will be related to your partner's health. Prepare in advance a plan for what you would do if things went wrong around the house or with your car. Usually, there is a simple avenue you can take to solve problem situations. A contingency plan just means that you do not have to worry about these matters in advance, and if they happen, you just have to refer to your plan. Even if you have to make slight adjustments at the time these things happen, at least you have some idea of what pathway you want to take.

A simple strategy to manage worry

It is a good idea to have a contingency plan, but that may not be enough to stop the pattern of worry that you have developed. To help control worry, you need to break the cycle of worry that leads to feelings of anxiety.

There is a fundamental difference between worry and problem solving. Worry involves you repeatedly going over the things you are concerned about without any useful outcome. Problem-solving is a means of identifying possible solutions, selecting your preferred problem-solving option and then implementing that strategy. A contingency plan is a means of outlining problem-solving options. In contrast, worry just take you around in circles.

Below is a simple strategy to control your worrying. It seems too simple to be effective but it has proved successful for many people.

Allocating worry time	
1.	Allocate a 15-minute period of your day for worrying. You choose the time that is more effective for you. For the purposes of this exercise, let's say you allocate 7.00-7.15 pm as your worry time.
2.	Throughout the day, catch yourself having worry thoughts. As soon as you notice you are worrying, acknowledge that you are worrying and tell yourself the following, "I will worry about that during my worry time, at 7.00 pm". Then deliberately move your thoughts to something else.
3.	Do this as often as you catch yourself worrying. Do not be concerned that when you start doing this, you will probably catch yourself worrying many times. Just remember that each time you notice you are worrying, remind yourself that you will worry about it at your allocated time and then move on to thinking about something else.
4.	When your allocated time arrives, you have permission to worry as much as you like for 15 minutes. However, you do not have to do this. Most often, people will not be bothered. You may also find that it is actually quite difficult to deliberately worry for 15 minutes. That is ok. You do not have to worry if you do not want to.

Exercise available at elemen.com.au

This will help stop the escalation of your worrying that leads to anxious feelings. However, there are many reasons why anxiety can be a constant companion when you are caring for your ill partner.

Manage your anxiety

Although a contingency plan might help you stop the cycle of worry, as will your new worry control strategy, it is likely that there will be times when you feel quite anxious. Learning to control your anxiety will help you feel much better and will improve the overall quality of your life. To learn to control anxiety it is necessary to understand how your nervous system works.

Functioning of your nervous system

Your autonomic nervous system (ANS) is the part of your nervous system that drives your functioning. It regulates your heart rate and temperature, and makes other adjustments that are required for you to function on a moment-by-moment basis.

Your ANS is divided into two parts: the parasympathetic nervous system and the sympathetic nervous system. Your parasympathetic nervous system is the part of your ANS that should be driving you most of the time. It makes sure everything is ticking along so that your body gets what it needs and you can function well.

Your sympathetic nervous system has a specialised function. It is your self-protection system that automatically activates when you are under threat. So, if you were crossing the road and a truck came screaming around the corner, your sympathetic nervous system would activate so that you could quickly and efficiently move out of the way of the truck and reach safety. Adrenaline would release into your system, causing your hands to shake and your heart rate to increase, but you would reach the safety of the footpath on the other side of the road, and you would be fine. Your brain would then recognise that you were safe, and your sympathetic nervous system would turn off, and your parasympathetic nervous system would take over again.

Your sympathetic nervous system is attuned to your brain perceiving signs of threat. It activates when you are at risk of harm and prepares you to deal with that threat. It is an effective self-protection system when you are under threat. Unfortunately, for people who develop an overly sensitive sympathetic nervous system or for people facing lots of demands in their lives, their sympathetic nervous system will activate at the slightest indication that something is wrong and will prepare you to deal with the threat. This can occur even when there really is no threat to manage. This is what happens when you are anxious in the absence of an obvious cause of your anxiety or an obvious sign of immediate danger. In effect, your brain cannot distinguish between an external threat (e.g., a truck coming around the corner) and an internal threat (e.g., you thinking worrying or anxiety-provoking thoughts). An overly sensitive nervous system will rely on its self-defence mechanism to protect you from perceived harm.

Your nervous system will react to crises in your life that do not present a threat of physical harm. Although the experience of increasing demands on you is stressful, it is not the same type of stressor as a truck about to run you down or a physical attack. Nevertheless, your sympathetic nervous system can be triggered by these ongoing demands. As stated, your brain cannot always make a distinction between an external threat to your physical integrity and the threat of persistent demands on your emotional wellbeing, the reaction to which is internally generated.

So, what effect does this have on you? Below is a table providing an overview of the activities of the parasympathetic and sympathetic nervous systems.

Table 2: The functions of the parasympathetic and sympathetic nervous systems.

	Parasympathetic	Sympathetic
Eyes	Constricts pupils	Dilates pupils
Salivary glands	Stimulates salivation	Inhibits salivation
Heart	Slows heartbeat	Accelerates heartbeat
Lungs	Constricts bronchi	Dilates bronchi
Stomach	Stimulates digestion	Inhibits digestion
Liver	Stimulates bile release	Simulates glucose release
Kidneys		Stimulates release of adrenaline and noradrenaline*
Intestines	Stimulates peristalsis and secretion	Inhibits peristalsis and secretion
Bladder	Contracts bladder	Relaxes bladder

* Also known as epinephrine and norepinephrine

When your sympathetic nervous system is activated, a series of physical changes occur that make sense if they are in response to a threat to your physical integrity. Some of those changes are listed below.

> Adrenaline is released so that you are alert and in a heightened state, ready to deal with the threat. This causes your heart rate to increase and can cause your hands, or even your whole body, to shake.

> Your hearing and your eyesight become better than normal. Everything sounds louder than it really is and you vision is more acute, making it difficult to tolerate

lots of light and movement. This is why anxious people tend to avoid places like supermarkets. Too much noise, too much light, and too much movement can be overwhelming when you feel anxious. Anxious people tend to tolerate these things poorly because of the acuteness of their senses when their sympathetic nervous systems are activated. It helps to have really good hearing and eyesight if you are being threatened, but it does not help if you are just trying to do your shopping.

The blood in your hands and feet is re-distributed to other areas so that you can do others things, such as, run really fast if needed. This makes your hands and feet feel clammy and cold which is an uncomfortable state to be in. When the blood returns to your hands and feet, you can get a tingly feeling that is also uncomfortable.

In our view, the most amazing thing that happens is that your sympathetic nervous system shuts down the systems you do not need to be using when you are reacting to threat. For example, when under threat, your body needs to produce lots of glucose for energy, so it stimulates glucose production. However, other systems that are not needed are shut down. In particular, your sympathetic nervous system shuts down your gastrointestinal system (e.g., inhibits digestion and inhibits peristalsis and secretion, with peristalsis referring to the contraction of the muscles that push forward the contents of your digestive tract). This is all right if it is shut down for the period of time it takes for you to deal with a truck coming around the corner. Your body copes less well with your gastrointestinal system not functioning if the sympathetic nervous system activation is prolonged. You can lose your appetite, experience nausea, develop diarrhoea or, less commonly, constipation, and you can experience difficulty eating, or you will overeat to try to control the uncomfortable state of your digestive system.

All of these symptoms make sense if you are under threat but become a problem if the activation of your sympathetic nervous system is prolonged. Also, when your sympathetic nervous system is activated for reasons other than an obvious threat, you can develop a sense of imminent danger just because your sympathetic nervous system has taken over your functioning. When your sympathetic nervous system is activated, your brain will interpret this as a sign that something is wrong. You will develop an overwhelming feeling that something terrible is about to happen even in the absence of an identifiable sign of threat.

Later, we will introduce some straightforward ways you can bring your sympathetic nervous system under better control so your anxiety and fear are reduced. You can learn to control the messages being received because you are worried or under pressure so that the message is not misinterpreted, and you can avoid that sense that something terrible is going to happen.

Range of arousal

As described earlier, it is likely that your sympathetic nervous system has been responding to your current situation as if it were an immediate threat to your physical integrity. When this occurs, you experience a number of physical changes that place your system into a self-protective state. You need strategies that will send a message to your nervous system that you are safe.

Before considering ways to achieve this, we need to look at one other feature of your nervous system. It is worth noting that human beings have a range of nervous system arousal within which we function the best. This range is quite large, from low in the range when we are very relaxed to high in the range when our nervous system is more 'revved up'. Pictured below is a diagram of this arousal range. The range within which you function best is known as the *window of tolerance*.

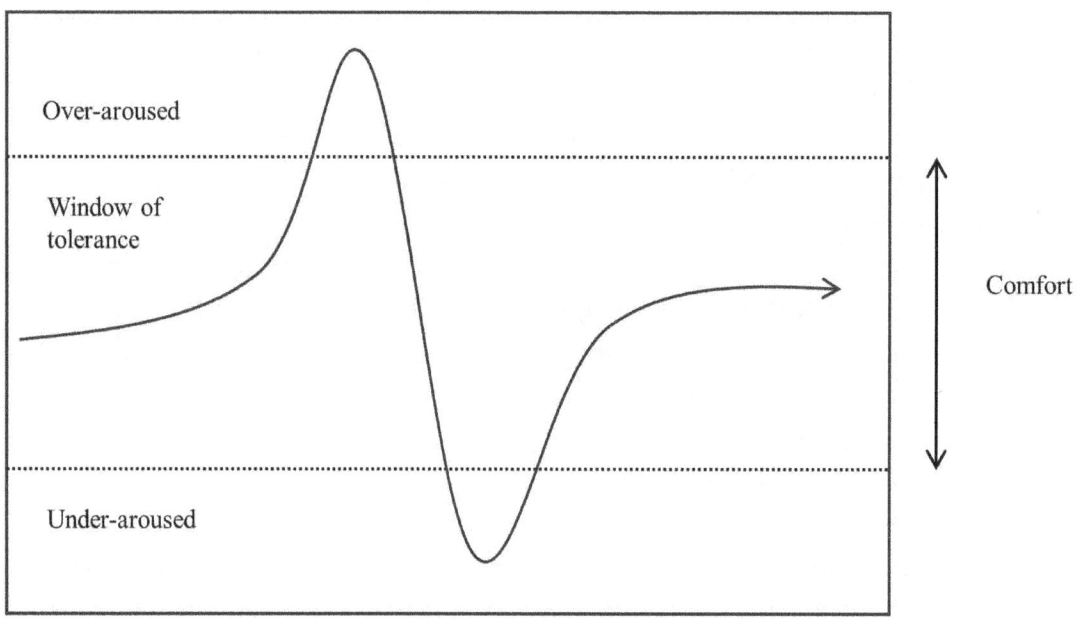

Figure 3: A diagram of the window of tolerance.

Within this window of tolerance, you have the flexibility to respond to the demands being placed on you. In this way, your arousal level will increase when you are faced with a demand and then decrease when that demand is over. As long as your arousal stays within this window, you will respond well to pressures placed on you.

If your arousal level drops below the lowest point of that range, you will enter a state of *hypoarousal*. In this state, you will feel slowed down and lethargic. Your functioning at this point will be inadequate, and your ability to respond to demands will be poor. If your arousal increases beyond the ceiling level, you will enter a state of *hyperarousal*. When this occurs, you can feel too aroused and can feel anxious and panicky. Your functioning will be impacted, and your ability to cope with pressures will deteriorate.

When you have been too stressed for too long or when you have been facing significant challenges but are still managing to cope, your arousal level creeps up from an optimal level of arousal in the middle of the window of tolerance to the upper extremes. You will find that you cannot or do not reduce that high level of arousal, even when you should be able to let go. This is why people cannot sleep well when they are under pressure. They can never relax enough for their arousal to decrease to a comfortable state. So, your 'baseline' arousal level, which is the starting point from which you respond to life demands, is high up in the range instead of midway.

In this case, your arousal level remains elevated. You barely notice this because it starts to feel normal to be under that much stress with your arousal level that high. But a problem exists. When any other thing occurs to which you have to respond, your arousal level will increase to deal with that additional demand being placed on you. However, when the starting point of your arousal level, or your baseline arousal level, is already so high, you have no room to move. Any increase in arousal will push you through the ceiling and into an uncomfortable and unpleasant hyperaroused state. You will experience anxiety as a result.

Your high starting point gives you no flexibility to respond or react to even minor additional stressors. So, the ways you normally cope with demanding situations fail because you have moved out of the range where you can successfully apply your usual coping strategies.

Anxiety management strategies

Your goal should be to get your nervous system back under control. Having too many demands placed on you or worrying too much about the future has likely pushed your arousal level to the upper limits of your window of tolerance. Extra demands, even minor ones, then cause your arousal level to move beyond the ceiling of the window of tolerance and uncomfortable and unpleasant anxiety symptoms are then experienced.

Optimal arousal level

You need to aim to bring your optimal arousal level down to at least the middle of the window of tolerance, with a baseline or starting point, when you are at your most relaxed, to the lower end of that range. Remembering that it now feels almost normal to have your nervous system so 'revved up', you need to retrain your nervous system to have a better starting point and a better optimal arousal level.

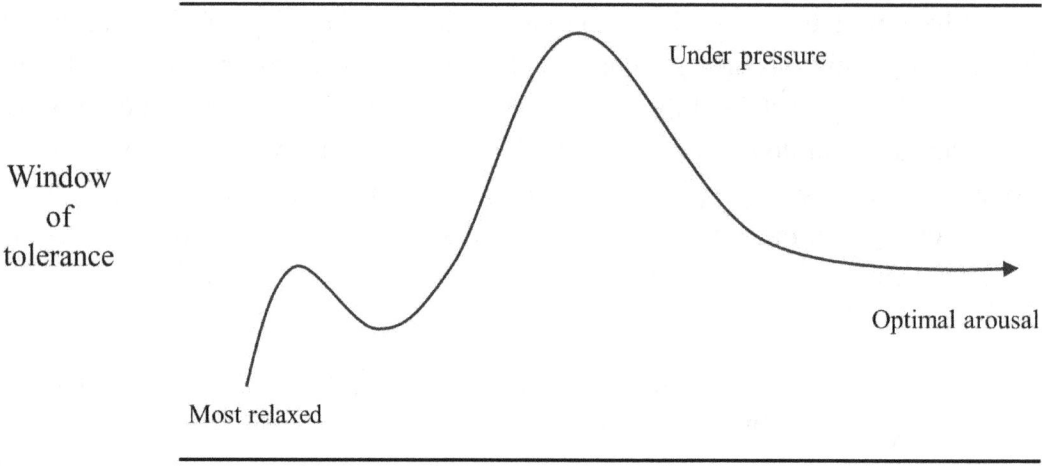

Figure 4: A diagram of an optimal arousal level.

Link between heart rate and breathing

How do you achieve this? Consider the following. When you are in an elevated or heightened state, at the top of your window of tolerance or beyond it, your heart rate increases and your breathing changes. Your heart rate elevation is caused by a release of adrenaline that occurs when your sympathetic nervous system is triggered. This can be very uncomfortable, and it feels like there is very little you can do about it.

Your breathing changes contribute to the elevation in your heart rate. When people are stressed, their breathing tends to be rapid and shallow. You can liken this pattern of breathing to the waves on top of the water. Form a picture in your mind of the way a child draws waves. When you are stressed, you tend to breathe in sharply, then breathe out quickly and then breathe in again quickly. You tend not to breathe all the way out before you breathe in again. This inhalation-exhalation pattern is what affects your heart rate.

In contrast, when you are relaxed, your breathing tends to be deeper and slower and has a pattern that is similar to the swell in the ocean. The inhalation-exhalation pattern is a comfortable breath-in followed by a long, slower breath-out. You do not breathe in again until you have breathed all the way out.

From the diagram below, you can see the pattern of anxious, rapid and shallow breathing on the top. Below that is the pattern of slower, deeper breathing that is characteristic of a more relaxed state.

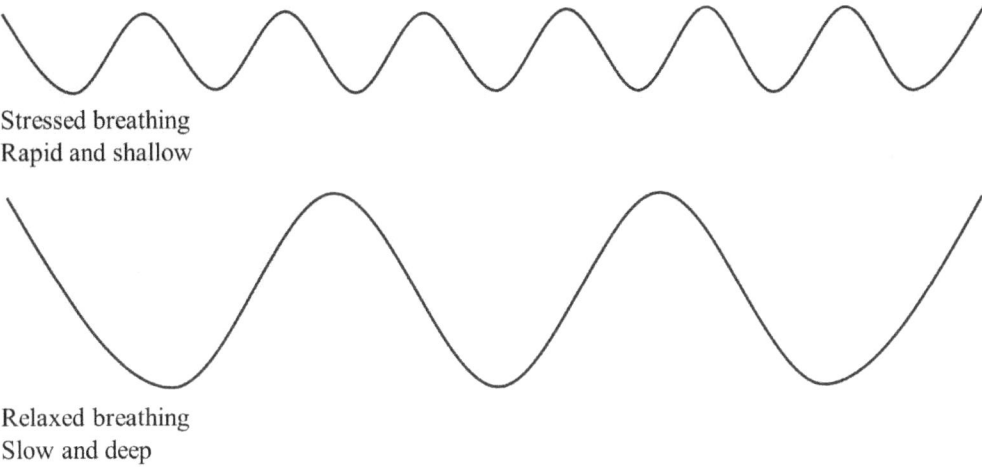

Figure 5: A comparison between stressed and relaxed breathing.

The reason your breathing pattern affects your heart rate is because these two things are linked. Under normal, stress-free conditions, your heart rate increases as you breathe in and then slows as you breathe out. This is normal. When you are stressed and your respiration rate increases and your breathing is shallower, your heart rate does not have a chance to slow before you breathe in again. Therefore, your heart rate is elevated and stays up.

Safety signals

Let's, for a moment, go back to the truck speeding around the corner, threatening to run you over. Your sympathetic nervous system is activated, allowing you to be in the right physical state to move quickly out of harm's way and protect yourself. When you get to the other side of the road, the truck goes past, and you are unharmed; your brain registers these experiences, and your sympathetic nervous system turns off, and your parasympathetic nervous system takes over. This is because reaching the other side of the road and seeing the truck pass you by are safety signals. Your brain interprets these signs as indicators that you are going to be all right.

Of course, no such safety signals are available when you are doing too much, sitting in your loungeroom worrying, or shopping at the supermarket. They are not that sort of event. Your brain would struggle to identify safety indicators because they do not exist in that sort of form. What you can do is offer your brain a safety signal but of a different type.

You can send a message that everything is all right by deliberately slowing your heart rate from its elevated rate to a more normal rate for you. Although it sounds difficult to achieve, that is controlling your heart rate, it actually is a reasonably straightforward undertaking. If you slow your breathing and lengthen your exhalation until you have breathed all the way out before breathing back in, your heart rate will come into line, and your heart rate will go down.

Breathing and muscle relaxation exercises

To use our waves and ocean swell analogy, the aim is to change the pattern of your breathing from waves on the top of the water to a pattern like the swell in the ocean, where the water is lifted up and then put back down as the swell passes. You are aiming for an easy, comfortable breath in, followed by a long, slow breath out.

The ideal situation is to breathe out for twice as long as it takes you to breathe in. Elongating your exhalation requires that you slow the amount of air you breathe out so that you can breathe out for longer. You should aim to breathe all the way out, emptying your lungs, before you gently and comfortably breathe back in.

This pattern of breathing should result in a slowed heart rate and a subsequent reduction in that sense of anxiety or crisis that occurs when your sympathetic nervous system is triggered. This occurs because your brain interprets the reduction in heart rate and the change in breathing pattern as a signal that the crisis is over. Below is a simple exercise you can use to slow your breathing.

	Slowing and controlling your breathing
1.	Without trying to change your breathing, just notice for a moment the pattern of your inhalations and exhalations.
2.	Now, take a comfortable breath in. It does not have to be too deep, rather just a comfortable breath.
3.	Now, breathe out, slowing the amount of air you exhale and lengthening your breath as a result.
4.	When your lungs feel empty of air, gently and comfortably breathe back in.
5.	As you breathe, practice lengthening your exhalation just a bit. You may also deepen your breath in slightly. Keep in mind the picture of the ocean swell if this helps.
6.	Practice this pattern of breathing for as long as you feel comfortable.

Exercise available at elemen.com.au

There is another element that you can add to this breathing exercise that may help with your ultimate goal of reducing your anxiety and signalling your sympathetic nervous system to turn off so your parasympathetic nervous system can do its job. You can include in this breathing exercise the element of reducing your muscle tension.

Reducing muscle tension

People who are stressed tend to have tense muscles. Although this muscle tension can occur anywhere in the body, common sites include the forehead and scalp, neck, jaw, shoulders, and chest. The increased muscle tension contributes to the overall sense of readiness to deal with threat. On the downside, tense muscles can cause headaches, chest and other pain.

If tense muscles present a significant problem for you, then a progressive muscle relaxation exercise may help. A general overview of this technique is provided below, along with a more comprehensive version. However, another easy strategy is to link the relaxation of muscles with the breathing exercise.

As you breathe out, just relax your muscles in places where they feel tight and tense. You do not have to achieve marked muscle relaxation to experience a noticeable difference. Just drop your shoulders, relax your jaw, smooth your forehead or relax your stomach muscles. Aim for a gentle relaxation of tight muscles as you exhale.

The combination of breathing exercise and muscle relaxation can be used even when the focus is on controlling your breathing. You can also use the combined technique when your primary focus is on troubling muscle tension. In combination, the techniques can help with either target.

	Combined breathing and muscle relaxation technique
1.	Take a comfortable breath in. It does not have to be too deep, but rather just a comfortable breath.
2.	Now, breathe out, slowing the amount of air you exhale and lengthening your breath as a result. As you breathe out, drop your shoulders, relax your jaw, smooth your forehead and relax your abdominal muscles.
3.	When your lungs feel empty of air, gently and comfortably breathe back in.
4.	As you breathe, practice lengthening your exhalation just a bit. You may also deepen your breath in slightly. Keep in mind the picture of the ocean swell if this helps. Continue to relax your muscles slightly on each exhalation.
5.	Practice this pattern of breathing and muscle relaxation for as long as you feel comfortable.

Exercise available at elemen.com.au

As stated, if muscle tension presents as a significant problem for you, you may wish to try a method of progressive muscle relaxation. This technique involves tensing and relaxing muscles progressively throughout your body. By doing this, you can learn to tell the difference between tense muscle and relaxed muscles. This is because, when you are tense much of the time, it starts to feel normal so it is hard to notice when you should be doing something about this degree of tension in your body. We will start with a longer version that will help you learn the technique. You can then change to a shorter version, which we describe below.

	Progressive muscle relaxation (longer version)
1.	Choose a comfortable place where it is quiet. Lay down or sit in a comfortable position with your feet flat on the floor.
2.	Now clench both your fists… tighter and tighter. Notice the tension in your muscles. Keep it clenched for about 10 seconds. Now relax. Feel your muscles relax. Notice the difference between the tension and relaxation.
3.	Repeat the procedure with your fists. Notice the difference between tension and relaxation.
4.	Now bend your elbows on both arms and tense your biceps. Hold the tension. Now relax. Notice the difference between tension and relaxation.
5.	Again, repeat the procedure with your elbows bent and your biceps tensed. Hold the tension, then relax. Pay attention to the change from tension to relaxation.
6.	Now, frown as hard as you can. Notice the tension in your forehead. Hold the tension. Now relax. Notice the difference you feel after you have released the tension.
7.	Now frown again as hard as you can. Hold the tension, then release it. Notice the contrast between tension and relaxation.
8.	Now close your eyes and squint them tightly. Hold the tension then relax. Allow your eyes to feel a comfortable relaxed state. Notice the change. Repeat by closing your eyes and squinting then relaxing, letting go of the tension.
9.	Now, clench your jaw. Bite down hard. Notice the tension throughout your jaw. Now, relax your jaw, allowing your teeth to fall apart slightly. Notice the feeling of relaxation. Repeat this exercise with your jaw.
10.	Now press your tongue hard against the roof of your mouth. Hold it there. Feel the tension at the back of your mouth. Now relax. Notice the difference between the tension and relaxation. Repeat the exercise with your tongue.

11.	Now purse your lips, pushing them out into an 'O' shape. Hold them there. Now release the tension and relax. Notice how your mouth feels now that it is relaxed. Repeat the exercise with your lips.
12.	Now press your head back as far as it will comfortably go. Hold onto the tension. Roll your head from the right to the left, allowing the focus of the tension to change. Now relax. Feel the difference between the tension in your neck and the relaxation. Repeat the exercise by pressing your head back.
13.	Now, bring your head forward with your chin on your chest. Feel the tension in your throat and the back of your neck. Hold the tension, then relax and allow your head to return to a comfortable position. Repeat the exercise by bringing your head forward.
14.	Now, shrug your shoulders, bringing your shoulders up and allowing your head to hunch down between them. Hold the tension. Now relax and notice the difference between tension and relaxation.
15.	Now breathe in deeply and hold your breath. Hold it. Now, allow yourself to gently exhale, letting go of tension as you breathe out. Feel your body relax. Repeat the exercise, breathing in, then gently letting go.
16.	Now tense your stomach muscles. Hold onto the tension. Now relax. Let your stomach muscles relax and appreciate that feeling. Repeat the exercise with your stomach muscles.
17.	Now arch your back without straining. Hold onto the tension. Now let it go. Notice the change in your muscles. Now repeat the exercise by arching your back.
18.	Now tighten your buttocks and thighs. Press down on your heels to flex your thigh muscles. Hold onto the tension. Now relax and notice the difference. Repeat the exercise.
19.	Now curl your toes downward to cause your calves to tense. Hold onto the tension. Now relax. Repeat the exercise.
20.	Now, draw your toes upward, causing your shins to feel tense. Pay attention to the tension. Now relax. Repeat the exercise.

21.	Now, scan your body. Notice if there are any tense spots. Repeat the exercise in that area.
22.	Enjoy the more relaxed feeling throughout your entire body. When you are ready, slowly return to your normal activities, holding on to that feeling of relaxation.

Exercise available at elemen.com.au

Once you have learned the technique, you can use a shorter version. You may prefer to just focus on the areas of your body that are particularly tense. It is certainly the case that some people tend to carry their muscle tension in one or two areas. Here is a shorter version that will allow you to tailor the procedure to suit your own needs.

	Relaxing using progressive muscle relaxation (short version)
1.	Choose a comfortable place where it is quiet. Lay down or sit in a comfortable position with your feet flat on the floor.
2.	Begin to work your way through groups of muscles by tensing them and relaxing them. For example, if you start with your forehead, tighten the muscles in your forehead by frowning. Hold for a few moments (10-15 seconds), then release, allowing the muscle in your forehead to relax, enjoying that experience for about 60 seconds. Notice the difference between the tension and the relaxation.
3.	Then, move on to the next group of muscles. You can work through groups of muscles from the top of your head to the tips of your toes, or you can select areas of your body that present a particular problem of tension for you.
4.	Repeat the process until you have worked your way through the groups of muscles you have selected.
5.	Repeat that process again, first tensing the muscles, holding that tension for five to ten seconds, and then relaxing those muscles.

Exercise available at elemen.com.au

So, controlling your breathing and, thus, lowering your heart rate will help you feel less anxious, as will reducing your muscle tension. However, there are other approaches you can take to anxiety management.

Quieting your mind

One of the problems with being anxious and 'revved up' is that your mind fills up with anxiety-provoking thoughts. When you have too much to do and too many things to worry about, you cannot seem to stop thinking in an endless stream of anxiety-provoking thoughts. This makes it very difficult to get your nervous system back under control. The thoughts racing through your mind do not allow you to relax. So, included here are some exercises that may help you settle your mind.

The first exercises aim to teach you to self-soothe. If you can learn to settle yourself, the racing thoughts in your mind may follow. The quieter your nervous system, the less active your mind is with anxiety-provoking thoughts.

What you are aiming to do is find ways to soothe yourself. Most of us can understand how we go about soothing an upset child. We might hold and rock a distressed child and say soothing things. What you are looking for are versions of self-soothing strategies for adults that will help to alleviate your distressed state.

The goal of developing self-soothing strategies is to create for yourself some moments of less distress. The strategies are aimed at reducing your heightened state to a more manageable level. They allow your nervous system arousal level to be brought back under your control. So, strategies that allow you to focus on the here and now are the ones that will allow you to choose to be in a quieter state with a greater sense of peace of mind.

Consider the proposed self-soothing strategies listed below and select ones that you think might assist you. These may be things you have tried before or ones you feel might work for you. Some of these strategies require you to make an effort to seek out the means of engaging with them. However, others are using things that are readily available or easily obtained.

	Self-soothing strategies
	Take a shower or a warm bath. Focus your attention on the sensations created by the water. Enjoy the feeling of the water on your skin and the warmth of the water. Turn your mind off to other thoughts and just focus on the water and its warmth.
	Play with your pet, or just stroke your dog's or cat's coat. Interacting with your pet has been demonstrated to be soothing for many pet owners.
	Change into your most comfortable clothes. Enjoy the feel of the fabric and the degree of comfort you feel from wearing these items of clothing.

	Go for a swim. Enjoy the sensation of being in the water. Allow those sensations to quiet your mind. Even if you are not a good swimmer, bobbing around in the water can produce the same sensations.
	Treat yourself to a massage if that appeals to you. Allow your muscles to relax and your mind to quiet.
	Listen to soothing music. Allow your attention to be directed to the music rather than have the music in the background.
	Listen to an audiobook, even if your distress makes it difficult to concentrate. Try to pay attention to each word that is spoken. If you lose track of the story, you can always return to the previous track and pick up the story again.
	Turn on the television or talkback radio and engage in listening to what is being broadcast. The goal here is to focus your attention on the conversations as they play out rather than selecting a programme you are excited to watch or listen to. It is the process of listening to others talking that is soothing.
	Listen to the sounds of water running. Again, the aim is to listen to the sounds of the water, stopping your mind from going to other intrusive thoughts. You can find the sound of running water in various places. You can visit a naturally occurring water course or waterfall. You could listen to running water from an outdoor garden fountain. However, you can also get an indoor personal fountain that can be used at any time. Alternatively, you can listen to recorded sounds of water running.
	Find something soothing to look at. This might be by the water or an outdoor space such as a park. It could be photographs or paintings that you find soothing or relaxing. The goal is to find something to look at that is engaging for you, and that you find relaxing and soothing.

Exercise available at elemen.com.au

Building on this notion of self-soothing, it is a good idea to be more present in your focus. If you give it some consideration you will find that the thoughts racing through your mind when you are anxious typically are not related to what is happening in the here and now. Our thoughts tend to engage in time-travelling, that is, they are focused either on what has already happened or what is to come. They rarely focus on what is happening in the present moment when you are trying to relax.

Usually, at these times, nothing is happening that is worth worrying about. If you could deliberately spend more time focused on the here and now and less time on the past or future, you would have a better chance of relaxing and quieting your overly stimulated nervous system.

The notion of focusing on the here and now is based on mindfulness techniques. Mindfulness refers to your ability to be aware of your emotions, your physical state, your actions and your thoughts in a state of mind that is absent from judgment or criticism of your experience. Research has demonstrated that mindfulness helps you to control symptoms of anxiety, to control the distress caused by particular situations, to increase your capacity to relax, and to learn how to cope better with challenging situations.

Based on the notion of mindfulness, we have included some exercises you can use to quiet your mind by focusing on the here and now. To do this well, you may need to practice the skill. When you first learn these techniques, it is easy to become distracted and return to your racing thoughts. Do not worry if this happens. Just return to your exercise and continue.

	Mindful listening
1.	Sit in a comfortable place, preferably by yourself. If you wish, close your eyes.
2.	Start to focus your attention on the sounds around you.
3.	Notice the changes in the sounds from moment to moment.
4.	Notice the times between sounds when it is quiet.
5.	Focus your attention both on what is happening inside and outside.
6.	Pay attention to the sounds and nothing else. Do not make judgments about the sounds. Just acknowledge the sound then listen to the next one.
7.	If thoughts about other things come into your mind, put them aside and then return to listening to the sounds around you.
8.	Do this for a few minutes or until you are ready to stop.

Exercise available at elemen.com.au

Let's try another mindfulness exercise.

	Mindful use of your senses
Sight	Look around you. Allow your attention to be drawn to five things in your immediate environment that you might not normally pay any attention to. For example, this might be the way the fruit is sitting in the fruit bowl, the way your curtain is hanging, or the way your books are placed on your bookcase. Allow your attention to rest on each of these things. Keep your focus directed at the item, setting aside any other thoughts that come into your mind.
Touch	Bring your attention to four things you can feel at this moment in time. For example, it may be the feel of the sun on your skin, or the feel of the fabric of your clothes against your skin, or the feel of the chair underneath you, or the feel of the table surface where your hand is resting. Allow your attention to rest on each of these feelings. Keep your focus directed at each sense of touch, setting aside any other thoughts that come into your mind.
Hearing	Listen to the sounds in your surroundings. Notice three things you can hear. For example, you might hear the sounds of cars travelling along the road, the noise of the refrigerator, or the sound of the wind in the trees. Focus your attention on each of these sounds. If other thoughts come into your mind, let those thoughts go and return to focusing on the sounds you can hear.
Smell	Pay attention and search for two things you can smell. For example, you might be able to smell whatever you are cooking, the scent of plants in your garden, or the sea air if you live near the water. Keep your attention focused on each of these smells. If other distracting thoughts come into your mind, let these thoughts go and return to focusing on the things you can smell.
Taste	When you are eating, focus your attention on the tastes you are experiencing. For example, take a sip of your coffee and notice the taste. Bite into your sandwich and notice the flavours. Really pay attention to the flavours of the things you are tasting. If you become distracted, let go of these interfering thoughts and return to focusing on the things you are tasting.

Exercise available at elemen.com.au

And there is one last mindfulness exercise.

	Mindful walking
1.	As you are ready for your walk, stand still for a moment. Sense the weight on your feet as you stand there. Feel how your muscles are supporting you and maintaining your stability and balance. Place your arms in a comfortable position of your choice (e.g., by your side or hands clasped, either at the front or at your back). Allow yourself to stand there, relaxed but alert.
2.	Begin to walk. Choose a comfortable pace, not too fast and not too slow. Pay attention to how your feet and legs feel (e.g., their heaviness or lightness, energy, or even any pain). The way your legs and feet feel will form the focus of your attention. If you become distracted, return to focusing on your legs and feet.
3.	Pay attention to the way in which you lift your feet and place them back down on the surface on which you are walking. Notice how you lift your foot, swing your leg and place your foot down again ahead of where you were a moment before. Walk in a natural and relaxed manner. Move your arms in a way that feels normal for you.
4.	It is likely that your mind will wander as you walk along. Your attention will be drawn to what is around you or thoughts that come into your mind. Acknowledge that you have been distracted and return to focusing on the process of walking… the lifting of your foot, the swing of your leg and the placement of your foot in front of you. Just gently return your attention to the sensations of walking.
5.	You might focus on a point ahead of you. Focus on the steps you take as you move towards that point. One step at a time. Experience fully the sensations of walking.
6.	Keep walking mindfully until you reach your destination or the point where you decide to turn around and mindfully walk back to where you started.

Exercise available at elemen.com.au

These types of strategies can help deal with the anxiety that is linked with repeated worry you may be experiencing about the stresses you are facing. There are also other ways to manage what your nervous system is doing. Let's consider the problem of anger.

Controlling your anger

It should be noted that there are times when your increased nervous system arousal will manifest as an angry response rather than an anxious one. You might find yourself raising your voice or becoming overwhelmed by frustration and annoyance. At these times, you can act in a way that does not make you feel good about yourself.

If you have a more significant anger control problem, then we recommend that you seek a workbook that focuses on more extensive ways in which you can learn to control your anger. However, here we would like to teach you a simple strategy to manage an angry response.

To understand why this strategy is effective, you need to consider that anger tends to be experienced in an escalating manner. That is an angry response is triggered and then gets worse when one or both of two things happen. The first is that you can think anger-provoking thoughts that will build your anger. These thoughts tend to relate to things not being the way you want them to be and your feeling that what you are experiencing is not justified and should not be happening.

The second refers to a process of reaction to how the other person responds to your anger that escalates the angry interaction. That is, a initial angry comment can be made, the other person then becomes angry, so you become more angry, then the other person's anger increases further. This escalating pattern leads to uncontrolled anger.

So, what should you do if you find your anger being triggered or escalating?

Exit and wait strategy

The most straightforward strategy you can use to stop the escalation of your anger and allow it to abate is an exit and wait strategy. When you are feeling angry, leave the situation and wait until you are calm before you return. It is an easy and effective strategy. Walk out of the room and allow yourself to calm down.

When away from the anger-provoking situation, there are a couple of tips you can use to help you calm down more quickly. Firstly, avoid going over the angry situation in your mind. This only aggravates your anger and makes it harder for you to settle down. So, when you leave the room, try to think about something else. Distract yourself by focusing on something that will hold your attention. Secondly, you can physically control your angry reaction by slowing your breathing and relaxing your tense muscles. This allows you to bring your nervous system over-arousal under control.

When you are calm and better able to handle the situation, return to what you were doing when the angry response was triggered. Go back with the right frame of mind. Decide that you are going to disengage from the interaction that caused the problem. You can adopt a spectator role by simply observing what you are doing without interpreting and judging. This will help you to continue while reducing the risk of further escalations of anger.

Manage your disturbed sleep

One of the consequences of your nervous system being revved up and having too many stressful thoughts is that your sleep can become disturbed. You can become fatigued as a consequence, and it becomes more difficult for you to cope with the demands of your day.

There are three types of insomnia. You might experience any one or all three of these types of sleep problems.

> *Trouble going to sleep.* This is where you are unable to go to sleep despite being tired.
>
> *Trouble staying asleep.* This is where you repeatedly wake throughout the night but, after a period of time, you are able to go back to sleep.
>
> *Waking early and being unable to go back to sleep.* This where you wake early in the morning and, despite needing more sleep, you cannot return to sleep.

Each of these types of sleep problems is understandable if you take into consideration your stages of sleep.

Table 3: A description of each stage of sleep.

Stages of sleep	
Stage 1	This is a transitional stage from wakefulness to sleep. It is associated with very light sleep. During this stage, muscle activity slows down.
Stage 2	During this stage, your sleep starts to deepen. Your breathing pattern changes and slows as does your heart rate. Your body temperature drops slightly.
Stage 3	It is at this stage that deep sleep begins to be experienced. To signal the onset of deep sleep, your brain starts to generate slow delta waves.
Stage 4	This is when you are most deeply asleep. During this stage, your muscle activity is limited.
REM sleep	This refers to Rapid Eye Movement sleep. It occurs when you are at the closest point to wakefulness. It is associated with vivid dreaming. During this stage, your heart rate increases.

Over the course of the night, you will cycle through these stages. For the first half or so of the night, you will cycle down into the deep sleep associated with stages 3 and 4. However, as the night progresses, the cycling pattern is lighter and does not involve deep sleep. This pattern is demonstrated in the diagram below. Periods of REM sleep occur at the point in the cycle when you are closest to waking.

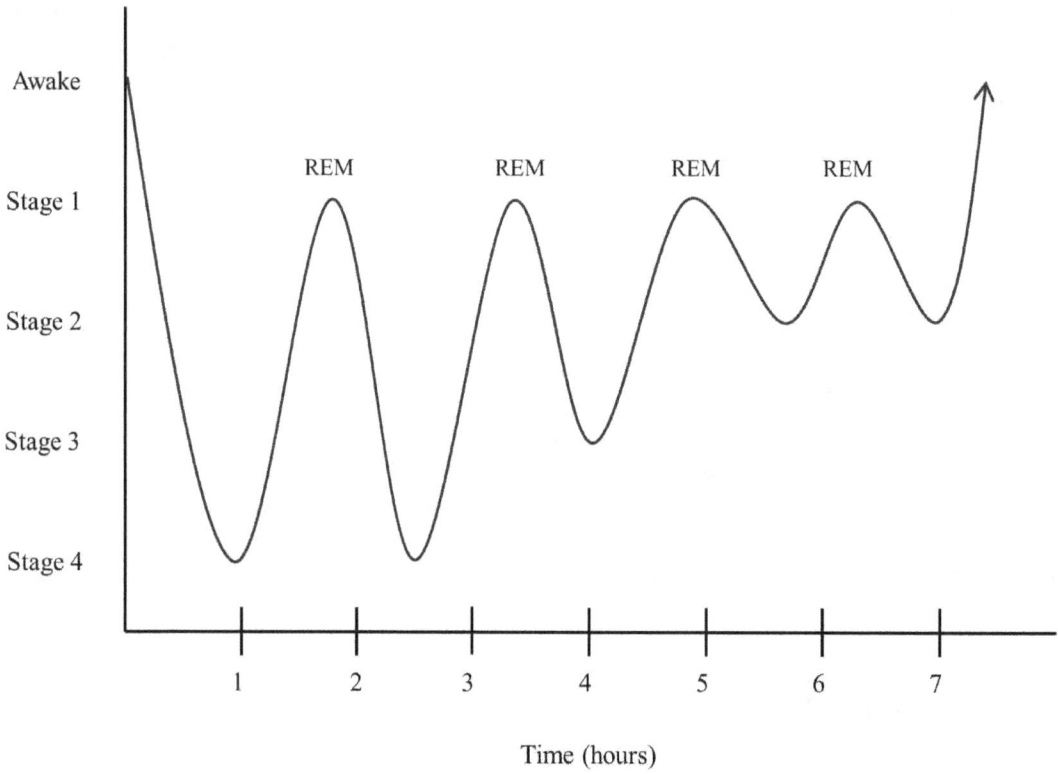

Figure 6: The cycles of sleep over the course of a sleep period.

When you have trouble falling asleep at the beginning of the night, you are struggling to enter into Stage 1 of sleep. This transitional stage is designed to pull you down into deeper sleep. Stage 1 allows you to do what your brain is inviting you to do, that is, sleep. Unfortunately, if you are stressed, your nervous system is generally too aroused to allow this to occur. Your nervous system fights against the urge to sleep. Your stressful thoughts are indicating to your brain that it is a good idea to stay awake in case something happens to which you need to respond.

When you have trouble staying asleep, you tend to wake up when your sleep cycle reaches those points where it is closest to wakefulness. In general, your nervous system is too aroused to allow you to stay asleep. Then, as soon as you wake, your mind turns to stressful thoughts that then keep you awake until you can get back to sleep. This can happen many times throughout the night.

When you are troubled by waking early and being unable to return to sleep, this usually occurs in the second part of the night when you have moved past the deep sleep cycles. Your sleep is lighter, and when your nervous system is too aroused, and you come close to wakefulness, you become completely awake, your stressful thoughts begin, and you cannot get back to sleep.

What can I do about my sleep problems?

Each of these types of sleep disturbance can be influenced by racing thoughts. These thoughts are usually of a stressful nature. They increase your nervous system arousal, making it difficult to get any rest.

Here is a series of simple steps that may help you have a better night's sleep.

	Simple sleep strategy
1.	In the evening, avoid caffeine and sugary drinks and food.
2.	In the lead up to your bedtime, start to wind down. Turn off stimulating television or stop engaging in other activities around the house that cause you to feel more alert.
3.	Have a small snack rich in carbohydrates.
4.	Get into a comfortable bed and into a comfortable position. Slow your breathing. Relax your muscle tension.
5.	Give your mind something to think about that is not emotionally arousing. This could be writing a simple story in your head, listing in your mind all the countries you can think of, starting with A, then B, etc. Count backwards by 7s from a randomly selected number.
6.	If your thoughts drift to more stressful thoughts, acknowledge what is happening and then return to the activity you chose to keep your mind focused.
7.	Allow yourself to drift off to sleep.

Exercise available at elemen.com.au

The goal here is to create the right sort of internal environment to facilitate a good night's sleep. Avoid caffeine and sugary food or drinks because they can have a stimulating effect on your nervous system. In general, you should be aiming to 'turn off' by reducing the number of external stimulating activities. You do these things in preparation for sleep.

Carbohydrates can also increase your readiness for sleep. This is because carbohydrates contribute to an increase in your brain of a protein called tryptophan. This is a building block for a neurotransmitter called serotonin and a hormone called melatonin. Serotonin has a role in controlling sleep, appetite and mood. Melatonin release is triggered by darkness, and this hormone helps promote a regular sleep-wake cycle. This process, triggered by eating a carbohydrate-rich snack before bedtime, helps you sleep.

When your mind is already overrun by thoughts that are keeping you awake, it seems counterintuitive to give your brain something else to think about. However, it is not the thoughts themselves that will keep you awake. It is the nature of the thoughts that will have an effect on your sleep. In this way, you want to distract yourself from thinking stress-related thoughts, replacing them with thoughts that will not cause you to react emotionally. You should aim to keep your brain busy with mundane thoughts so that your mind is distracted from the stress-inducing thoughts. We like to refer to this activity as 'busy work' for your brain. It is the modern-day equivalent of counting sheep.

Mundane thoughts will allow you to drift off to sleep, whereas stress-related thoughts will keep you alert and awake. Your brain is always active so it is not possible to stop thinking. When you think of things that cause your nervous system to respond by increasing your arousal, you will have trouble sleeping. If you think calming or even boring thoughts, your brain will trigger the processes that lead you to falling asleep.

The same strategy of giving your mind something other than stressful things to think about can be applied if you awaken during the night. Simply get settled and focus on the mundane thoughts you have selected, allowing yourself to drift off back to sleep.

Learn acceptance

When you are dealing with the deteriorating health of your partner, you are faced with ongoing changes. Most of these changes are not things you would choose to have happen. This can cause you to experience distress when the changes occur and even after they occur.

To cope with this you need to consider a change in attitude to one of acceptance rather than being tormented by events that you cannot change. There are lots of things that can happen that cause you pain and emotional upset. The more you focus on these situations, the more distress you tend to feel. The goal here is to learn to accept the things that you cannot change.

Often when we have to deal with a change we did not want, we tend to get upset thinking that this is something that should not have happened, or should not have happened to you or to your partner. Rather than battle events that have already occurred in this way, the goal is to accept that they *did* happen and that it is now appropriate for you to deal with these changed situations.

Being distressed about a situation does not help you cope with that situation. It is a fact that you cannot change the past. Nevertheless, we tend to emotionally react to these situations as if there is something we can do to change them. In doing this, you become stuck and do not look for other, more effective ways of coping with your new circumstance.

In learning acceptance, you need to acknowledge your changed situation without trying to control it or change things that have already happened. Try to understand that your current situation has occurred because there was a long chain of events that occurred in the past that brought you to this point. Your job now is to use your coping skills to move forward with life, as it is a waste of your energy and effort to torment yourself thinking "if only…" or "what if…".

This type of acceptance does not mean that you cannot wish that things had turned out differently. It also does not stop you from looking for ways to manage or improve your current situation or avoid things that might happen in the future. This type of acceptance is asking you to look at your situation and accept it for what it is. It is from here that you can then choose what you want to do about it.

Whenever you feel overwhelmed by your situation, you can use simple coping statements that will remind you that a position of acceptance is preferable. Consider the following coping statements. Add any that you can think of that would help you accept what has happened so that you can move forward and deal with things as they arise.

	Acceptance coping statements
	Below are some examples of coping statements you can say to yourself that would help you achieve acceptance. These coping statements remind you to accept your situation and the events that contributed to your current situation. Tick the coping statements that you would find useful, and then add any others you believe will help. Then, when you feel overwhelmed, use these coping statements to help you manage your reaction to the events that are stressing you.
☐	Things are the way they are.
☐	There is a chain of things that contributed to what is happening now.
☐	I cannot change things that have already happened.
☐	There is no point battling past events.
☐	Battling the past upsets my present.
☐	I can only deal with the present.
☐	It is a waste of my energy to try to change the past.
☐	The present is as it should be, even if it is not what I would choose.
☐	This moment in time has occurred because of all the things that came before.
Add your own coping statements	

Checklist available at elemen.com.au

These coping statements can remind you to stop fighting a past you cannot change. This will free you up to accept what has happened and then focus your energy on moving forward and doing what is best for you. Acceptance of what has happened invites you to cope with what you are experiencing.

Manage your emotional reactions

Before we move on to learning how to improve and take advantage of your coping skills, it is worthwhile to spend some time learning about ways to control your emotional reactions to stressful events. This will help you achieve acceptance of your situation, allowing you to feel more settled and less distressed.

Primary and secondary emotions

Emotions are the reactions we have to the things that happen to us or the things we think about. When something good is happening, you will feel pleasurable emotions, and you will respond positively to your situation. When something bad is happening, you will experience distressing emotions, and you will view your situation negatively.

Human beings can experience a full range of emotional responses from strongly negative to strongly positive. However, as human beings, we are complex creatures with the capacity to experience a range of emotions as a result of any one event. Sometimes, this can be overwhelming. It then makes sense to be able to regulate your emotions so that the emotional state you are in does not overwhelm you.

Let's consider how we react emotionally. Initially, when something happens, we experience an emotional response. These initial responses are referred to as *primary emotions*. They are the reactions we have to our experiences.

However, as we are complex individuals, we can then develop an emotional reaction to our initial emotional reaction. These emotions are referred to as *secondary emotions*. Secondary emotions refer to the feelings we have about our feelings. Let's consider an example. You go to the cinema with a friend to see a movie. The content of the movie makes you feel sad, and you burst into tears. Then, afterwards, you feel embarrassed that you felt so sad and cried in front of your friend. The sadness you felt about the movie was your primary emotion. It was your initial reaction to what was happening. The embarrassment you felt was your secondary emotion. This was the feeling you had in response to your primary emotion.

Our secondary emotions can become quite complex. Consider the following example.

Examples of complex emotions	
What happened?	*I had a nasty argument with a family member.*
How do you feel?	*I feel sad* (primary emotion).
How do you react to this feeling?	*I don't like feeling sad, and I want it to go away.*
What do you say to yourself?	*"What if I can't stop being sad?"* *"What if this sadness continues to affect my relationship with my family member?"*
What do you feel then?	*I feel anxious* (secondary emotion).
How do you react to this feeling?	*I don't like the feeling, and I want it to go away.*
What do you say to yourself?	*"Now I feel anxious, and I can't cope."* *"I am stupid for feeling anxious when it was just a family disagreement."*
What do you feel then?	*I feel self-critical* (secondary emotion).
How do you react to this feeling?	*I feel uncomfortable and stressed.*
What do you say to yourself?	*"I am stupid for feeling this way."*
What do you feel then?	*I feel annoyed with myself* (secondary emotion).

So, instead of just feeling sad, you now feel sad, anxious, self-critical and annoyed. Your primary emotion is sadness, and all the rest are secondary emotions.

One way to stop this process is to focus your attention and coping efforts on your presenting emotional state. For example, if you feel sad then give this emotion your attention and work on ways to cope with your sadness. The sadness you are feeling is your primary emotion at that time. It is the emotion you feel directly because of what has happened to you.

Your emotional reactions can be difficult to manage because what started as a straightforward emotional response to a stressful event turns into a confusing array of emotions. Sometimes, these emotions can compete with each other and pull you in different directions. For example, you can feel both sad and angry, or angry and excited. Trying to deal with one of these emotions can be undermined by your efforts to deal with the other emotion.

There is a need to simplify things when you are dealing with difficult situations. You can learn to focus on your primary emotions as they arise and adopt strategies to deal with them. Let's start by looking at a way to identify your emotions so you know what you should be giving your attention.

Recognising and dealing with your emotions

There is a need to simplify things when you are dealing with difficult situations. You can learn to focus on your primary emotions as they arise and adopt strategies to deal with them. Let's start by looking at a way to identify your emotions so you know what you should be giving your attention.

Let's start by taking the process of experiencing an emotional reaction a step at a time.

What happened?

Here, consider the situation that developed that resulted in you feeling these strong emotions. Identify specific details of what happened rather than talking in generalised terms (e.g., "I never cope", "I always make mistakes").

Why did this situation occur?

Consider the possible causes of the problem situation. This is an important step. It gives you the opportunity to interpret the meaning of the problem situation in an effort to help you understand why you are feeling the strong emotions you are experiencing.

How were you feeling as a result of that situation?

Try to identify your primary emotional response to the situation and then consider the secondary emotions you experienced as well.

What is it that you wanted to do *as a result of how you were feeling?*

Here we are referring to the urges or impulses you have to act in response to the emotional state you are in. When feeling strong emotions, people tend to experience urges to do more extreme actions.

It does not follow that you will always do these things. However, thoughts about doing them can be present. It is worth noting that people tend to *think* about doing extreme things much more often than they ever *do* them. What this means is that you control the impulse to act in an 'over the top' way. If you can control these impulses, you can control others in a way that will allow you to have a more settled and reasonable response to provoking situations.

What did you actually do and say?

Here, you are considering what you actually did rather than what you had an urge to do.

After experiencing those emotions and actions, how did they affect you?

Here, we are referring to the consequences for you of experiencing those strong emotional states and your reactions to those states by choosing to act in a particular way.

To try and make sense of what you are feeling and why you are feeling it, we suggest you use the worksheet below. It is designed to help you understand how you are reacting to the problems you are facing, and this may direct you to how you can cope with the situation. First, let's look at how you can use this worksheet.

Understanding your emotions worksheet - example
Time and date: *Wednesday 8th.*
What happened? *I realised I have to take on the care of the garden which used to be my husband's job.*
Why did this situation occur? *The deterioration in my husband's condition has caused him to lose strength, resulting in me having to take on jobs around the house that he used to do.*
How were you feeling as a result of that situation? *I was feeling anxious* (primary emotion) *that I would not be able to take on another big job around the house. Having to feel anxious because of this extra burden just made me feel resentful* (secondary emotion) *that I have been so overburdened.*
What is it that you wanted to do as a result of how you were feeling? *In response to feeling anxious about being overloaded, I had the urge to run away and hide and not return. In response to feeling resentful, I had the urge to scream out loud.*

What did you actually do and say?
In response to feeling anxious, I found a quiet place in the house and had a little cry. In response to feeling resentful, I have just tried to ignore the feeling and push on with what I had to do.

After experiencing those emotions and actions, how did they affect you?
I felt overwhelmed and withdrew as a consequence. This may have caused me to be less responsive to my husband's needs for a period of time.

Below is the worksheet you can use.

Understanding your emotions worksheet
Time and date:
What happened?
Why did this situation occur?
How were you feeling as a result of that situation?
What is it that you wanted to do as a result of how you were feeling?

What did you actually do and say?

After experiencing those emotions and actions, how did they affect you?

Worksheet available at elemen.com.au

The link between your emotions and your behaviour

In learning to focus on your primary emotion and resolve that emotion so that the secondary emotions can be avoided, it is worthwhile understanding the link between your emotional state and the things you choose to do in response to that emotion. This is important. It is difficult to control your behaviour choices if you do not appreciate the link between how you feel and what you do.

Let's consider how you might behave in relation to your emotional responses. Consider the example of the person who reached the point where she realised she would have to take on the gardening because her husband could not do it any longer.

I felt	What I did
Anxious	*I found a quiet place in the house and had a little cry.*

Understanding this link between your emotional state and your behaviour can help you learn to make different choices in how you act when you are upset. We will explore this further when we consider building your coping strategies, but let's consider here how you might opt to do different things. Consider the same example, but now let's look at how this person might have chosen to do things differently.

I felt	What I did	What I could have done instead
Anxious	*I found a quiet place in the house and had a little cry.*	*I could have looked into how much it would cost to get a gardener to help or investigate whether I could access gardening help through community services.*

Let's take this one step further and consider the likely outcomes of the initial behaviour choice and the alternative one.

I felt…	*Anxious*
I did…	*I found a quiet place in the house and had a little cry.*
What happened?	*I just felt even more anxious that things seemed so hopeless that all I could do was cry.*
A better choice…	*I could have looked into how much it would cost to get a gardener to help or investigate whether I could access gardening help through community services.*
Likely outcome…	*My anxiety would have vanished because I had a plan of action. I would have realised that I had some options to explore, and this would have made me feel hopeful.*

Initially, you can work on thinking up alternative and healthier behaviours after the event. This will allow you to learn how to make better choices by considering the different outcomes of various behaviours. It will then become easier to apply this strategy when you feel the emotional reaction so that you can choose the better behaviour at the time and avoid doing things that might feel all right at the time but do not help you in the longer term. Below is a worksheet you can use.

The emotion-behaviour link worksheet	
I feel/felt…	
I did/I felt the urge to do…	
What happened/ what would have happened?	
A better choice…	
Likely outcome…	

Worksheet available at elemen.com.au

Remember, here, your goal is to focus your attention on your primary emotion. If you can resolve your primary reaction to the problem you are facing, then other secondary emotions may either not occur or simply resolve. When you experience secondary emotions, tell yourself that you are going to focus your energy on your primary emotional reaction. You can then give your attention to finding ways to cope with the triggering source of your distress.

Here you have learned to identify your emotional reactions and to respond to them differently, focusing on your primary emotions and responding to your urges to act in a different way. Now we need to focus on building your coping skills so that you can choose to do particular things that will help you overcome difficult times.

Find ways to cope

We are going to examine ways you can cope. We will explore the fact that people have preferred styles of coping, and your best chance of coping well is to build up your coping strategies in the way that best suits you. Let's start to explore coping in general and your preferred coping style.

Coping

We all have our own coping resources and individual coping skills. Coping resources are the things we have available to us to help us cope, such as family relationships and friendships. Coping skills are the strategies we are good at that we use to deal with the problems we face. We have our own particular coping resources and specific coping skills because there is not one particular way of coping.

In a general sense, the way you will cope with the problems you are facing in relation to your partner's deteriorating health will likely be a reflection of the way you have dealt with and solved other problems throughout your life. That is, the way you cope will reflect your general style of coping.

Your goal should be to understand how you cope and to make good use of the coping resources you have or can create, as well as the particular skills you have developed or can develop. This is true even if you take into account the fact that dealing with your partner's deteriorating health may be a more challenging problem than other problems you have dealt with in your life. For those of you who feel you do not cope well with life problems, it may be the case you have been trying to develop coping skills based on a pattern of coping that does not suit you.

To understand the way you cope and to use this knowledge to choose the best strategies to cope with your partner's deteriorating health, consideration needs to be given to the fundamental differences people can have in the way they approach problem situations. Let's consider the different approaches to coping so that you can work out your own preferred coping style.

Problem-focused coping vs. emotion-focused coping

To start, a distinction can be made between problem-focused coping strategies and emotion-focused strategies.

Who are problem-focused copers?

Problem-focused copers deal with their problems by considering the problem situation and trying to fix it. They tend to want to *do* something when they are confronted with a problem. They are most comfortable when there are specific things related to the problem that can be the focus of their attention. In the context of a partner's deteriorating health, problem-focused copers are the ones who will look for ways to control the situation, such as searching for and investigating new treatment options.

Who are emotion-focused copers?

Emotion-focused copers are the people who deal with their problems by expressing their emotional reactions to the situation. They will talk about the problem and cry when they feel the need. They see the value of looking to others to share their feelings about their problem. In the context of a partner's deteriorating health, the emotion-focused coper will cry and talk to a friend about how they are feeling.

Are people either emotion-focused or problem-focused copers?

Some people are strongly problem-focused copers, and some people are strongly emotion-focused copers. Others fall somewhere on the continuum between the two extreme positions. You may be more problem-focused than emotion-focused, but still make use of some emotion-focused strategies… or the reverse.

You will be able to do a little exercise to find your coping preferences or to confirm them if you already have a good idea of where on the continuum you fall. But, first, we have to consider one other element.

Problem-approach vs. problem-avoidance copers

People assume that when we talk about coping strategies, we are referring to good ones that will help us deal with the problems we face. This is not the case. People's coping style can be divided on the basis of whether they tend to front up to their problems or whether they prefer to avoid them. This is the case for both problem-focused copers and emotion-focused copers.

Let's start by looking at problem-focused coping. How would problem approach and problem avoidance strategies differ? Consider the examples in the table below.

Table 4: Examples of problem-focused approach and avoidance strategies.

Problem-focused, problem approach strategies	Problem-focused, problem-avoidance strategies
Problem-solving Problem-solving coping strategies involve: Examining the problem Generating potential solutions Evaluating the likelihood of a successful outcome Moving forward and applying the strategy	*Problem avoidance* Problem avoidance coping strategies involve: Deliberately avoiding thinking about the problem Deliberately avoiding reminders of the problem
Cognitive restructuring Cognitive restructuring coping strategies involve: Reframing your thoughts to think more reasonably about the problem Correcting errors in thinking that are barriers to coping with the problem	*Wishful thinking* Wishful thinking as a coping strategy involves: Wishing the problem would go away Indulging in thoughts that things will return to 'normal' Spending time thinking about how things will work out in your favour and as you wish

With regard to your partner's deteriorating health, effective, problem-focused approach coping strategies may help in the following ways. They may help you generate ideas of how to solve specific problems you face, such as accepting additional home help. They may also help you to work out ways that you can cope more effectively with the demands being placed on you, such as deciding that it is acceptable to take some time out for yourself.

Now, let's consider emotion-focused coping. The table below details examples of approach and avoidance emotion-focused coping strategies.

Table 5: Examples of emotion-focused approach and avoidance strategies.

Emotion-focused, problem approach strategies	Emotion-focused, problem-avoidance strategies
Emotion expression Emotion expression as a coping strategy involves: Being open and talking about how you are feeling Allowing yourself to experience your emotional reactions in relation to the problem Using emotional expression as a form of catharsis, letting off steam to allow yourself to feel better for a while	*Self-criticism* Self-criticism as a coping strategy involves: Blaming yourself for the problem Criticising yourself for failing to control your emotional reaction to the problem Viewing yourself as more generally deficient than is warranted
Social support Using social support as a coping strategy involves: Turning to family and friends for support Talking with your support network about how you are feeling Taking comfort from your support people Allowing your support network to offer instrumental support	*Social withdrawal* Social withdrawal as a copy strategy involves: Cutting yourself off from family and friends Failing to seek professional support when it is needed Refusing assistance offered by the people who wish to help you or would be willing to do so

When we consider your partner's deteriorating health, effective emotion-focused approach coping strategies may be of assistance to you in the following ways.

They may allow you to express your emotional reactions and deal with them rather than bottle them up. They may result in you choosing to seek support from carer organisations or counselling professionals or from your family and friends to allow you to discuss how you are feeling and, potentially, resolve some of those feelings that can be overwhelming if they are kept hidden.

Identifying your preferred coping style

The goal here is to identify the type of coping that works best for you. If you are an emotion-focused coper, you may see the value of a problem-focused coping approach, but it is unlikely that you could comfortably adopt problem-focused coping strategies and expect them to work for you. Your efforts would be better directed at taking advantage of your preferred style of coping, using problem-approach strategies.

Here is an exercise in determining what type of coping style best characterises your preferred type. Tick the boxes if you typically use the listed coping strategy.

	How do I normally cope?
Problem-solving	
	I work on finding ways to solve the problems I face.
	I work out what I should do, and then I follow the plan.
	I like to work out a plan and then move forward.
	I believe there is a solution to every problem.
Problem avoidance	
	I try to act like nothing is wrong.
	When faced with a problem, I choose not to do anything, even when I know I should.
	I try not to spend any time thinking about the problem.
	When the problem comes to mind, I push it out of my head.
Cognitive restructuring	
	I think about my problems in a way that allows me to realise I can manage them.
	I think about the problem to change the way I react to it.
	I try to look on the bright side of any situation.
	I try to put things into perspective.

Wishful thinking	
	When faced with a problem, I just wish it would go away.
	I just hope a miracle will happen to make everything all right.
	I hope the problem will fix itself.
	I wish that someone would come and fix the problem for me.
Emotion expression	
	When faced with a problem, I allow myself to express my feelings about it.
	I do not try to bottle up my feelings; I let them go so that I can feel better.
	I do not hide my feelings about the problem from other people.
	When faced with a problem, I just need some time to experience my feelings.
Self-criticism	
	I blame myself for the problem I am facing.
	I ask myself what I have done to make the problem happen.
	I tend to hold myself responsible for the problems I face.
	When a problem occurs, I feel I should have done things differently.
Social support	
	I turn to the people I know will listen when I talk about how I feel.
	I feel better when I can talk to others about my problems.
	When faced with a problem, I seek advice from people I trust.
	I allow other people to offer help and support when I am dealing with a problem.

	Social withdrawal
	When faced with a problem, I like to avoid other people and spend time by myself.
	When I am struggling with a problem, I do not want to be around other people.
	I do not share my thoughts and feelings with others.
	I do not accept the help others offer.

Checklist available at elemen.com.au

What type of coper are you? Add up the ticks you have placed in each of the categories and enter the number in the following table.

Ways of coping score sheet	
Problem-focused strategies	*Emotion-focused strategies*
_____ Problem-solving _____ Cognitive restructuring _____ Problem avoidance _____ Wishful thinking _____ **Total**	_____ Emotion expression _____ Social support _____ Self-criticism _____ Social withdrawal _____ **Total**
Problem-approach strategies	*Problem-avoidance strategies*
_____ Problem-solving _____ Cognitive restructuring _____ Emotion expression _____ Social support _____ **Total**	_____ Problem-avoidance _____ Wishful thinking _____ Self-criticism _____ Social withdrawal _____ **Total**

Score sheet available at elemen.com.au

When comparing your problem-focused and emotion-focused strategies, see where you have scored the highest. This may show a strong preference for one type of coping strategy or the other. If so, you can build on your preferred coping type when you consider what coping strategies will help you with your current situation. If you have similar totals for both problem-focused and emotion-focused strategies, you would do best to include each type in your coping plan.

When considering whether you use problem-approach strategies or problem-avoidance strategies, you are considering whether adjustments have to be made in the way you cope. If you predominantly use problem-avoidance strategies, you can learn to abandon those in favour of problem-approach strategies while staying within the same style of coping strategy, that is, problem-focused or emotion-focused.

Building your coping repertoire

Now that you better understand the ways you cope, you can start to build a plan of how you are going to move forward, adopting coping strategies that work for you. Let's consider some examples of coping strategies you could adopt.

Problem-focused strategies

We will start by looking at problem-solving strategies. Here you are trying to work out a plan of how you would go about solving a specific problem situation, followed by decision-making with regard to which potential solution you would choose. You then should be able to follow through and solve your problem.

Let's consider an example of this process.

Example of a problem-solving strategy
What is the problem? Clearly define the problem you are facing. *The problem I am facing is that I have too many things to do and not enough time to do them all. I have become overwhelmed by all the demands that have been placed on me.*
Generate as many possible solutions as you can. List the ones that are likely to work. *I could do the following:*   *I could just keep doing what I have been doing and hope I can find the time to do everything.*   *I could get someone to come in and help, such as a community support worker.*   *I could learn to manage my time better and prioritise things that are important.*

Consider the likelihood of each of these strategies being successful.
If I keep doing things the way I have been doing them, it doesn't seem likely that this would work. I am already exhausted, and I just don't see how I can keep up the pace for an extended period of time. It doesn't seem likely that I could do this without burning out and becoming unwell myself.
I could investigate what assistance is available through community services. If I could get some homehelp and this person did some of the housework, for example, this would free me up to do some of the other things on my list of things to do. With the help of someone else, the number of things I have to do would lessen.
I could prioritise things differently. The trouble with this idea is that learning time management skills would probably just free me up to take on more jobs. If I was able to get more time, I would prefer to use that time to do some things that are enjoyable, such as some leisure time for me. I might be able to generate some more time but the number of jobs I have to do wouldn't reduce.
Select the problem-solving strategy that is likely to work the best.
I choose to explore getting some home help through community services. This is the option that would both reduce the number of things I have to do and give me more time to do some things for myself which I need.
What are you going to do next?
I am going to contact community support services to see what services are available to me. I will make an appointment to talk to them about my needs.

In this example, the person has thought about the problem and identified possible options for resolving it. The person then considered what the likely outcome for each possible solution would be. They then chose their preferred solution and worked out a plan for their next step. This is a good problem-solving approach.

Here is a problem-solving worksheet you can use.

Problem-solving strategy worksheet
What is the problem? Clearly define the problem you are facing.
Generate as many possible solutions as you can. List the ones that are likely to work.
Consider the likelihood of each of these strategies being successful.
Select the problem-solving strategy that is likely to work the best.
What are you going to do next?

Worksheet available at elemen.com.au

Now, let's consider a cognitive restructuring approach to coping. A cognitive restructuring strategy focuses on the way you are thinking about a problem. Below is an example of a cognitive restructuring approach to addressing a problem situation.

Example of a cognitive restructuring strategy
What is the problem? *I have so much to do that I am not able to do things to the standard I would normally expect of myself.*
What are you thinking? *I think I am not doing a good enough job. People might think I am not doing a good enough job looking after my partner.*
What evidence do you have that this is true? *I usually set high standards, but I have not been able to achieve this.*
What evidence do you have against this being true? *Things are getting done. My family and friends actually tell me I am doing a good job.*
Even if it was true, what is the worst thing that would happen? *Well, nothing really. I only have to please myself and my partner.*
What do you conclude? *I am probably doing a good enough job, given the difficult circumstances I am facing. My partner is being looked after, and that is the most important thing. It doesn't really matter what other people think because they are not in my position.*

Here, the person in this example challenged the way they were thinking about their situation. Then, they examined whether the situation was as bad as they were interpreting it to be. Having realised that was not the case, they then worked out a better and more realistic way of thinking about their problem. You can see that their alternative thoughts about their situation would make it easier for them to cope. They were tormenting themselves with thoughts that they are not good enough. Instead, they could be more accepting of their situation and realise that it is not something they really have to worry about.

Below is a worksheet you can use to consider a cognitive restructuring coping strategy.

Cognitive restructuring strategy worksheet
What is the problem?
What am I thinking?
What evidence do I have that this is true?
What evidence do I have against this being true?
Even if it was true, what is the worst thing that would happen?
What is my conclusion?

Worksheet available at elemen.com.au

Emotion-focused strategies

Next, we will consider how to enhance your emotional expression coping skills.

Example of an emotion expression strategy
What is the problem? *We got more bad news at the doctor's appointment the other day. The latest scans showed the cancer hadn't reduced despite treatment.*
What did you do? *I tried to pretend that everything was all right. I stayed cheerful so that my partner wouldn't become upset.*
What were the advantages of doing this? *I don't really know. I just felt like I was pretending… I <u>was</u> pretending. My partner also knew I was pretending, so I didn't even protect them.*
What were the disadvantages of doing this? *I felt like my head was going to explode. I felt like I was going to fall apart. I worried that if I fell apart, there would be no one to care for my partner. I was scared about what was going to happen.*
What could I have done differently? *I could have expressed how I was really feeling about the news. I could still have comforted my partner and found time to deal with my own reaction to what we learned.*
What would the advantages have been of doing things this other way? *I would have felt some relief. I wouldn't have felt like my head was about to explode, and I would have got rid of the knot I felt in my stomach. If I had dealt with my emotions, I would have reached a point where I could get on with things sooner than was the case, having bottled everything up inside.*
Would there have been any disadvantage of doing things this other way? *Not that I can think of. My partner already knew I was only pretending to be cheerful.*
What will you do next time you feel like this? *Next time I will be honest about my emotions and express them in a way that lets me manage the news better.*

In this case, the person went through a process of examining the pros and cons of both not expressing their emotions and expressing their emotions in response to the news they received. The conclusion was reached that the better option was to allow themselves to react in a genuine way to what they were feeling.

Below is a worksheet you can use to develop emotion expression coping strategies.

Emotion expression strategy worksheet
What is the problem?
What did I do?
What were the advantages of doing this?
What were the disadvantages of doing this?
What could I have done differently?
What would the advantages have been of doing things this other way?
Would there have been any disadvantages of doing things this other way?

What will I do next time I feel like this?

Worksheet available at elemen.com.au

Finally, we can consider how to use social support as a coping strategy.

Example of social support as a strategy
What is the problem? *Being so focused on caring for my partner and doing everything I have to do at home has made me feel isolated and lonely. My partner is too ill to be much of a companion.*
What have you done in response to this problem? *I have pushed my feelings to one side and just tried to get on with things. I have told myself that there are more important things to think about than my loneliness.*
How has responding in this way helped you with your problem? *Well, I don't suppose it has. I can push thoughts about my loneliness out of my head for short periods of time but it hasn't actually changed my lonely feelings at all.*
What could you do instead? *I could reach out to my family and friends and let them know how I feel.*
How would this be likely to work out? *I think my friends and family would be likely to do the best they could to help. They really care about me... and I care about them. I think they would arrange to spend time with me and catch up more. I think they have not been doing that already, only because they thought I was too busy or that they would be interfering.*
So, what are you going to do next? *I am going to take the time to phone a friend to catch up for a chat.*

Here, the person thought through their situation and realised they were doing the opposite of what they should have been doing to fix their problem of loneliness. They realised the solution was available to them, and there were advantages to pursuing the solution. It was an easy step then to follow through with their plan and reach out to others.

Below is a worksheet for you to use with a social support coping strategy.

Social support strategy worksheet
What is the problem?
What have I done in response to this problem?
What could I do instead?
How would this be likely to work out?
So, what am I going to do next?

Worksheet available at elemen.com.au

In moving forward, remember to choose the coping strategy that best suits your preferred coping style. Always choose approach strategies rather than avoidance strategies, no matter what your coping style.

Manage your time

From what we have discussed so far, it is apparent that one of the problems you can face is having too much to do and too little time to do it in. As a result, it is worth considering some time management strategies.

Let's start by considering the list of things you need to do. We can work out ways to approach this list.

Prioritise what you need to do

Not everything on your list of things to do is of equal importance. However, we do not always take this into consideration when we are trying to get things done. We will, in effect, waste time doing unimportant things when much more important things are waiting for our attention.

When you make a list of the things you feel you need to do, divide the items into:

Important items: These are the things you must get done most urgently.

Somewhat important items: These are things that you will need to get around to doing within a reasonable amount of time.

Unimportant items: These are things that could be left as it does not really matter if they are done.

You should aim to do the important items first, followed by the somewhat important items and, finally, the unimportant items if you have time to get around to them. Let's look at an example of a list of things to do that has been re-prioritised in this way.

We can look at the list of a person, Kelly, who has a list of things she needs to do. She is a working mother who is also caring for her husband who has a degenerative disease. Let's examine what she has put on her 'to-do' list.

Kelly's list of things to do	
1.	*Sort out power of attorney for my husband.*
2.	*Complete the enrolment form for a drug trial for my husband.*
3.	*Phone to accept position in drug trial.*
4.	*Go to the supermarket.*
5.	*Take children shopping for new shoes.*

6.	*Clean out the linen cupboard.*
7.	*Finish the report at work.*
8.	*Arrange a meeting to discuss the next project at work.*
9.	*Update contact list at work.*
10.	*Meet with stakeholders about possible outcomes of the current project.*
11.	*Pay the phone bill.*
12.	*Replace the annoying tap in the laundry.*
13.	*Reorganise the pantry.*
14.	*Attend social event at children's school.*
15.	*Reassign duties to take advantage of workers' expertise and take into account their preferences.*
16.	*Return best friend's message.*

Now, we can prioritise these things that Kelly feels she has to do. We can do this by dividing the list into three lists based on the importance of each item.

Prioritisation of things to do - example		
Highly important	Moderately important	Less important
Phone to accept position in drug trial. *Complete enrolment form for drug trial for my husband.*	*Sort out power of attorney for my husband.* *Go to the supermarket.* *Take children shopping for new shoes.* *Finish the report at work.* *Arrange a meeting to discuss the next project at work.* *Pay the phone bill.* *Meet the stakeholders about possible outcomes of current project.*	*Clean out the linen cupboard.* *Update contact list at work.* *Replace the annoying tap in the laundry.* *Reorganise the pantry.* *Attend social event at children's school.* *Reassign duties to take advantage of workers' expertise and take into account their preferences.* *Return best friend's message.*

In this new, re-jigged list of things to do, Kelly has two highly important things to do. Both of these tasks relate to her husband's health and, in particular, the drug trial into which he has been accepted. Once these things have been done, Kelly can move on to her next list.

Although the 'moderately important' list is longer, it is largely related to three things. There is one item related to securing the future by organising power of attorney. There are a number of items regarding work. In effect, these tasks are related to moving from one project at work to the next. The other items relate to the smooth running of the household and the care of the children. The items in this category will impact others if Kelly does not get around to doing them.

The items that are less important are on Kelly's wish list but there will be no real consequences if she takes a while to get around to them. Although there might be advantages in getting them done, there is no real urgency for these things to happen.

Below is a prioritisation worksheet you can use to sort out the things you have to do in terms of their importance or urgency.

Prioritisation of things to do		
Highly important	Moderately important	Less important

Worksheet available at elemen.com.au

Break down your high priority, important tasks

Sometimes, items on your important list can seem overwhelming. You may tend to avoid doing them by filling in your time with less important tasks just because the important items feel too difficult. One way to overcome this is to break the items into more manageable steps. Each of these steps can seem less overwhelming. If you work through the steps, you end up achieving your goal of completing the important item.

Consider the following example.

Examples of steps to complete an important task	
Task to be completed	*Completion and submission of an application form for support services.*
Steps	*Gather documents and identification I need.* *Read through the form.* *Complete the form in sections.* *Check I have included everything necessary.* *Submit electronically or by mail.*

Avoid distractions and deals

It is an easy trap to fall into to avoid doing the things that are important by allowing yourself to be distracted. These distractions usually are of less importance than the task you should be undertaking. Remember, complete the most important tasks before moving onto less important tasks.

It is also a form of avoidance to make deals with yourself, such as, "I will complete the support services form after I have dusted the bookcase". These deals are designed to make it acceptable to not do the thing you must do but least want to do. Of course, even if you do undertake a less important activity, the most important one still remains.

How to make time when you seem to have none

When you start learning time management techniques, it can seem impossible. In particular, it seems inconceivable that you can make time when none seems to be available. It feels like there are not enough hours in the day to do all you need. However, it is possible to make time if you follow some rules.

There are four 'must do' rules for making time. These include:

Learn to say no.

> Even when you are overwhelmed, and people understand this, you can still be asked to do more. It is all right for you to put your needs over those of other people's less important needs. You can do this even if you are the sort of person who would normally want to be of assistance to others. It just takes an understanding that sometimes your needs are greater than the needs of another person. In fact, it is not possible for it to be any other way. Just ask yourself, "Whose need is most important?". When you learn to comfortably say no, you can find extra time that you would normally devote to unnecessarily doing things for other people.

Ignore the unimportant items on your to-do list.

> These items on your to-do list should only come to your attention if you have completed all of your important and somewhat important tasks. Remember, they are rated as unimportant because they can be left without any undue concern. Indeed, these are the sorts of tasks that can be handed on to other people to do. In an understanding of the demands on you, your family and friends may ask if they can help you. Learn to feel comfortable handing on unimportant tasks when these offers are made. This will buy you more time, and it will help the people who genuinely care about you feel that they are doing something useful to assist you.

Make reasonable time estimates.

> When you are working out how long it will take you to do things, try to make a realistic estimate of how long each task will take. Things typically take longer than

you think because when we make an estimate, we do not take into account interruptions or events we do not expect. So, do not try to squash into the day as many tasks as you can in the shortest period of time. If you do this, you will become increasingly frantic and frustrated at not getting everything done, and these feelings tend to interfere with your productivity. Usually, you can do more if you pace yourself well and remain focused.

Build relaxation time into your schedule.

For the very reason that you make more progress if you approach your tasks in a paced way, you should build into your day rest times when you can relax. Frantically moving from one task to the next will exhaust you and slow you down as the day progresses. You would be better off setting aside rest times that should only be interrupted by emergencies.

There are other rules you can follow if you choose. These are not necessary but may help you manage your time better and produce time when none seems to be available. Consider the following options and identify those you might try to use.

	Possible time generating ideas
	Generate a short list of brief tasks (5 minutes) that you can do while you are waiting for something else to occur or if you find yourself with a few moments before you start your next important task.
	Learn to multitask. You can think about doing one thing while you do another.
	Hand on your unimportant tasks to others.
	Do an additional task while you are watching television. For example, you can watch television and fold the clean laundry.
	Stop using avoidance and distraction strategies when you are faced with an important task.
	Time-limit activities that are not productive when there are important tasks to do. For example, talk to your friend when they telephone you, but not for half an hour.
	Put things back in their place as soon as you have finished with them. That is, do not leave things lying around. You will just have to find time to put them away later when the task of putting away multiple things will seem like a bigger one.
	Turn your back on perfectionism. You have to get things done. These things do not have to be done absolutely perfectly.

Checklist available at elemen.com.au

One of the benefits of managing your life better, is that you can have more time available for yourself. Let's consider next how you should use that time.

Increase your life satisfaction

It is important that you have the opportunity to do some things for yourself. Having a balance between the tasks that are important that you must undertake and some leisure time will improve the balance of your life.

With limited time available to you, it is important that you choose activities that are meaningful to you and will improve the satisfaction you feel with your life. It is easy to fill your life with things to do, even leisure activities. However, not all of these potential activities will give you a sense of satisfaction. This is because not all activities are important to you. If you are going to use your precious time, you should choose an activity that is of high value to you.

How do you know what activities would contribute the most to improving the quality of your life? We often do not think about what we value as we go through our busy day and the question of what a person values can often be confounding to them. Borrowing from a particular therapy called Acceptance and Commitment Therapy, we have included here an exercise in values clarification that will help you decide which activities would be of the greatest value to you.

The goal of this exercise is to identify ways you can put into your life the things that you value the most. The purpose of doing this is to improve your quality of life by having more things in your life that matter to you the most.

When we refer to the things you value, we are not referring to a specific activity. For example, you may have a value related to spending more time with your family. A specific activity that might flow from this value is to have a meal with your family once a week.

Below is a diagram that contains labels for various life domains. A life domain is an area of your life that reflects one portion of who you are and what you do. This is an example of what we are talking about when we refer to your life domain map.

Values clarification exercise for choosing preferred activities

Step 1 involves you listing as many life domains as you can think of that are relevant to you. We have included some life domains that people often list, but feel free to change them and add new ones that are relevant to you. What you are doing here is building your life domain map. Take your time to think up as many life domains as you understand to be part of your life. Other examples might be travel, intellectual pursuits, exercise, etc.

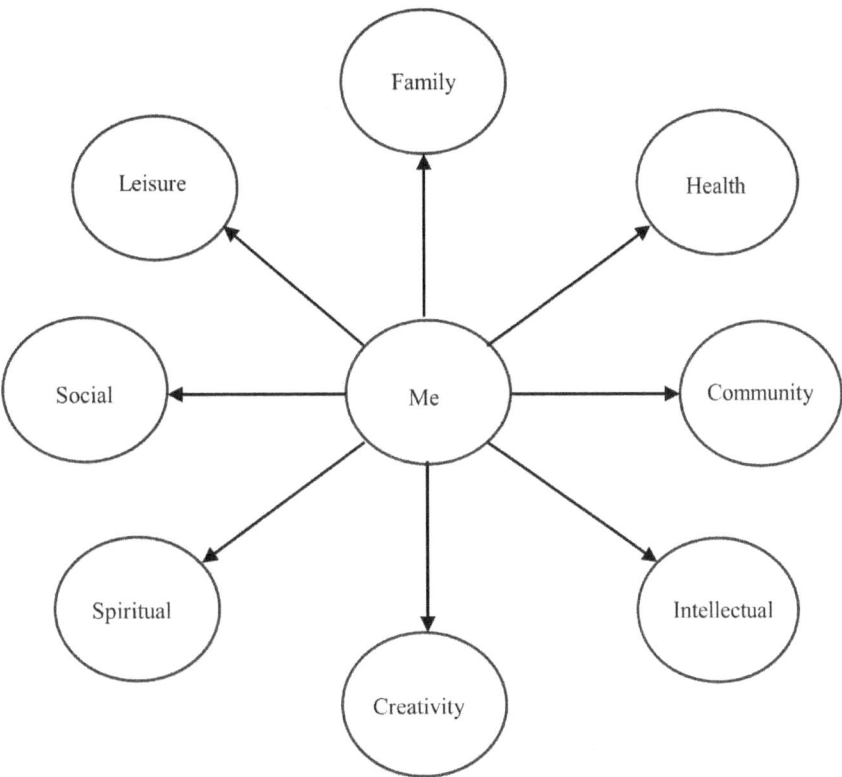

Figure 7: Example of a life domain map.

Step 2 involves you identifying what you already have in your life for the various life domains. Remember, list the values you have (e.g., ample time with my family) rather than specific activities (e.g., Sunday lunch with my family). You will begin to notice that some domains in your life have received lots of attention, but other domains have received little or no attention. Here is an example of the types of values that might appear in the family domain.

    Family domain:

        Time with family

        Special time with individual family members

        Spending time with the young members of my family

        Important family gatherings

Remember, you are listing here what you already have of value in your life with regard to this domain. This is not a list of the things you would like to have available to you.

Step 3 involves you now considering the things you would like to have in life in each of the domains. Again, focus on the values (e.g., more quality time with my parents) rather than activities (e.g., visiting my parents on Sunday afternoons).

At this point, you will begin to notice several things.

> You will see that there are domains of your life that have received lots of attention already, and you want very little else in that domain. Things in these domains are already satisfactory, so there is limited purpose in focusing your attention on them.

> You will see that there are domains of your life where you have very little but you also do not really want very much more. These do not deserve your attention either.

> Importantly, you will see there are domains of your life where you have very little, and there are many things that you want in that domain that you do not already have available to you. Focusing your attention on these would give you the greatest benefit.

It is the third type of life domain that will become the focus of attention from here on. This is because this focus will have the greatest chance of having the most important impact on the quality of your life.

Step 4 involves focusing on those life domains where you do not have enough of what matters to you, and there is very much more that you want to include in your life. In this step, you should consider how those values that you want to put into your life might translate into specific activities. It is here that the 'what to do' component of the exercise occurs. For example, if you have a value associated with spending more time with your family, you might now consider ways that could happen by identifying specific activities you could engage in that would bring that value into your life (e.g., arranging family get-togethers, organising an online shared family photo site where family members can post photos for all family members to see).

Step 5 involves identifying any barriers that might prevent you from engaging in these activities that would bring the things that you value into your life and finding ways around these barriers. For example, you may not be able to catch up in person with family members if they live in places distant from you, but you could overcome this barrier by arranging online chat get-togethers.

Of course, there will be things you want that are of value to you that you just cannot have because of real limitations. For example, you may like to travel, but you cannot because your partner is very unwell. However, if travel is of high value, then the quality of your life might be enhanced by spending time exploring places online or watching travel documentaries. Although not exactly what you would give the highest value, these activities are still related to the thing that matters to you.

Remember that your goal is to introduce activities that are of high value to you that will improve the quality of your life. If you are going to devote the time to engaging in these types of activities, it will matter that you focus on the activities that are associated with your highest values.

Need for self-care

Here, we want to make a short comment about the importance of self-care. It is important, not only because of your own wellbeing but because you need to be well and coping effectively to be able to care for your partner. We wish to make a number of points.

Do not ignore your own physical health. You need to stay as well as possible for yourself and your partner.

It is not selfish to take some leisure time. You need to have a balanced lifestyle so that your wellbeing and good adjustment is maintained.

Do not be self-critical about feeling disappointed, frustrated or resentful sometimes. These are normal human reactions to stressful events. In any case, it is not whether or not you experience these emotions; it is how you learn to deal with them that matters.

Try to take charge of the things you can control and, let go and accept the things you cannot control. By doing this, you will develop a better sense of being able to do the things you set out to do. Continually focusing on the things you cannot control will leave you feeling helpless, and life will feel overwhelming.

Accept help when it is available. Seek it out if it is not offered. You do not have to develop a complicated justification for accepting help. If you are feeling overloaded or that you have too much of a burden to carry, then it is reasonable to accept assistance.

We wish you all the best.

Additional reading

Clark, D.A., & Beck, A.T. (2012). *The anxiety and worry workbook: The cognitive behavioral solution.* New York: The Guilford Press.

Devine, M. (2018). *It's OK that you're not OK: Meeting grief and loss in a culture that doesn't understand.* Australia: St Martins Press.

Eifer, G.H., Forsyth, J.P., & Hayes, S.C. (2005). *Acceptance and commitment therapy for anxiety disorders.* New York: New Harbinger Publications.

Kubler-Ross, E., & Kessler, D. (2014). *On grief and grieving: Finding the meaning of grief through the five stages of loss.* US: Scribner Books.

Tobin, D., Holroyd, K., Reynolds, R., & Wigal, J.K. (1989). The hierarchical structure of the Coping Strategies Inventory. *Cognitive Therapy and Research, 13(4),* 343-361.

www.ingramcontent.com/pod-product-compliance
Lightning Source LLC
Chambersburg PA
CBHW080856090426
42735CB00014B/3169